The Girl in the Painted Caravan

EVA PETULENGRO

with Claire Petulengro

PAN BOOKS

First published 2011 by Pan Books
an imprint of Pan Macmillan, a division of Macmillan Publishers Limited
Pan Macmillan, 20 New Wharf Road, London N1 9RR
Basingstoke and Oxford
Associated companies throughout the world
www.panmacmillan.com

ISBN 978-0-330-51999-1

1 3 5 7 9 8 6 4 2

A CIP catalogue record for this book is available from
the British Library.

Typeset by Ellipsis Books Limited, Glasgow
Printed in the UK by CPI Mackays, Chatham ME5 8TD

Visit www.panmacmillan.com to read more about all our books
and to buy them. You will also find features, author interviews and
news of any author events, and you can sign up for e-newsletters
so that you're always first to hear about our new releases.

The Girl in the Painted Caravan

Eva Petulengro is a member of the last generation of true Romany gypsies. She spent her childhood on the road with her family in their beautiful painted caravan, before going on to become one of the country's leading clairvoyants and astrologers, with many famous clients. Today she lives in Brighton near her three sons, Warren, Bradley and Gregory, and her daughter Claire, who followed the family tradition and is a popular astrologer and author.

For Mummy, my brother Eddie, and Johnnie,
the love of my life, who inspired and encouraged me
to put pen to paper and finally tell my story

Contents

Prologue

I was born in a painted caravan in 1939, into a Romany family who had travelled the roads of Norfolk and the Lincolnshire fens for generations. It was a way of life we loved, rooted in traditions that had given Romanies a strong sense of pride in ourselves and our unique culture for centuries, but which could not withstand the changes of the twentieth century. Although its time was passing I was lucky to have experienced its old ways, to be lulled to sleep by the patter of rain on the caravan roof as I lay warm in bed, hearing my brothers and sister breathe nearby. To have sat around the camp-fire laughing and talking as dinner cooked, the tang of woodsmoke mingling with the smell of the meat and herbs to make your tummy rumble with hunger.

What I miss most of all is waking up in a new town with new adventures to be had. We moved to Brighton and into bricks and mortar when I was twenty-one, forced off the roads as travelling became too difficult.

We told ourselves it was just for the season, that we would soon be moving on again. We never did. Fifty years later, I still live in Brighton. But even now, in my seventies, every few years I wake up and know it's time to move on, even if it's just down the road. I need to find somewhere new to make my home. When you're born a Romany, you will always remain a Romany.

This is the story of my childhood and my heritage. It's the story of a time when we could roam freely through the countryside; of love and laughter, excitement and disappointment, innocence and mischief; and of the wonderful, and not so wonderful, people we met on our many travels.

The way we lived means that written records of our past are few and far between, so I relied solely on my memory and that of my relatives as I put pen to paper. Not a day goes by when I don't think back on my childhood with fondness, and I've laughed a lot and cried just as often as I've remembered the events that have made up my life so far. I hope the following pages give you a glimpse into how we really lived as the last generation of true Romany gypsies. It is a way of life, now largely relegated to the pages of history, that I am very lucky to have experienced.

ONE

All You Need is Love

'Eva, gal, you look beautiful,' Mummy says, her whole face lighting up with pride as she sees me all dressed up to the nines.

I'm wearing a shocking-pink georgette blouse, a pencil skirt and five-inch heels. My black hair is in its usual French plait and huge gold hoops hang from my ears. I look polished but inside my stomach is doing somersaults of anticipation. It is 24 October 1964 and the Beatles are in town. They are playing tonight at the Brighton Hippodrome and the organisers have given me permission to go backstage to meet them. Word on the street, though, is that no one is going to be allowed in and that it's every man, or woman, for themselves. We'll see about that, I thought. I hoped my press pass and my ability to charm people would be enough to get me in.

'Where's that Nathan gone?' my mother frets. 'He should have been here by now.'

EVA PETULENGRO

Nathan is my younger brother by three years, and he's also my cameraman, bodyguard and best friend all rolled into one. Before we can start to debate what's happened to him, the door bursts open and a dead ringer for Tommy Steele walks in. Nathan has the same fair curly hair and cheeky smile and is dressed in a smart navy-blue suit, white shirt and winkle pickers. Around his neck is a paisley dickler, a silk scarf which most Romany men choose over a tie for special occasions.

'Are you ready, gal?' he demands. 'Let's get a move on. It's packed out there.'

I put on my black jacket with the mink collar and rush to the mirror, digging in my bag for my black eyeliner. With a practised hand, I go over the line I drew on earlier in the day – a little more can never hurt. Finally ready, I make my way to the door.

'See you later, alligator,' I shout to Mummy.

'In a while, crocodile,' she smiles. Then she stands and cocks her head to one side. 'Just a minute,' she whispers. She rushes into the bedroom and returns very quickly with something in her hand. As she empties the contents onto my palms, I look down. 'No, Mummy,' I gasp. 'You can't.'

'Yes, I can,' she says assertively and looks me squarely in the eyes. She has placed my grandmother Alice Eva's gold charm bracelet in my hands. I know

4

this means the world to her. 'Granny is as proud of you as I am. You've done good, Eva, and you need to know that. Here, it's yours now.'

With this, she turns on her heels, walks back into the kitchen and starts singing along with Dean Martin on the radio. As I shut the door, I notice that she's wiping a tear from her eye. Mummy is not a woman who shows her feelings very easily and this makes me realise how far we've all come. I know that bracelet meant the world to Granny and to Mummy and now it's mine. As I join the clasp round my wrist, I feel more grown up than ever before. But Nathan brings me back down to earth with a bang. 'Move it, rabbit's arse.' He grabs my arm and we're off, pounding down the stairs from our first-floor flat. By now I am feeding off his excitement.

We walk down West Street and turn onto the seafront. I love the smell of the sea, mixed with the vibe of Brighton, but tonight there is something especially surreal about the atmosphere, a sense that the town is buzzing. As I look out at the waves crashing onto the beach, I wonder where my Johnnie is now, and if he's thinking about me and missing me as much as I'm missing him.

As we turn onto Ship Street, we see it is mobbed with the kind of crowd you get before a football match. People are pushing and shoving forward, trying to get to the Hippodrome, which is at the other end of the road. But it seems much further than that now, from where we are standing. I'm determined the crowd is not going to stop us.

Nathan holds his camera bag in front of him and pushes his way through the screaming girls. This works and so I follow closely behind. We manage to get as far as a little alleyway called Ship Street Gardens when Nathan turns round with a worried look on his face. 'We can't get down there, it's absolutely choc-a-block.' We are forcibly being pushed towards the Heart in Hand pub as the crowd elbows past us desperately. 'I need a pint. Come on, let's get in here,' he sighs with resignation.

Even this seems like an impossible challenge when we push open the door to the public house and realise how many other people had the same idea. It is heaving in there! Luckily for us, we know the landlady. She recognises me and beckons me over, ignoring the people at the bar shoving notes her way in the hope of getting some more drinks down their throats.

She passes me a tomato juice and Nathan a pint and then, with a wink, she mouths the words 'There's some people in the back who will want to meet you'. This is not abnormal when I come in here. The regulars know I'm a clairvoyant and often have the Dutch courage to pose questions they'd usually be too shy to ask. We push and shove our way through to the back room, which is kept for the stars who are in town, or people from the theatre who want to relax and have a drink in peace.

As we walk in, I don't recognise anyone. Nathan pulls at my shoulder. 'Check out over there. It's that band, Sounds Incorporated,' he whispers. I don't have a clue who they are. Suddenly a young man appears by my side and puts his hand out. 'It's a bit hot in here, ain't it?'

'I was hoping to interview the Beatles, but we can't get through,' I blurt out, my disappointment clearly showing.

With a wry smile, he says, 'Well, we've got to get through, because we're supporting them!' A rush of adrenalin shoots through my body. We've got an in, an impossible in, I think to myself. 'These guys are doing our security,' he adds, nodding towards a group of well-built men. 'They'll get us through.'

We quickly down our drinks and, with a few hurried whispers and some winks and handshakes, the security guards daisy-chain around us and start moving us through the pub. 'Security, security,' they shout, pushing the girls and guys in front of us out of the way. Part of me starts to feel slightly sorry for the array of faces around me, being shoved aside so determinedly, but the thought that we might make it backstage to meet the

Beatles pushes such worries to the back of my mind.

Nathan's eyes lock with mine and we smile. 'Fina,' we both say at the same time, which in Romany means good. With that, we start laughing.

Out of the front door, we find ourselves moving up the street and, slowly but surely, we reach the stage door of the Hippodrome. The poor souls who have managed to make it this far are pushed very firmly out of the way and we stand in their place, waiting for the doorman to vet us and see if we are one of the favoured few allowed to gain access to the band. They spot the lead singer of Sounds Incorporated and the door widens. 'Come on in, guys,' they shout. They don't need to ask us twice.

Once inside, we are faced with yet another crowd, this time made up of reporters and photographers. They turn around to see who we are. 'They're not seeing any press,' says someone I know from the *Daily Mail*. Then I spot Annie Nightingale, a local DJ and writer. She has obviously been waiting a long time and says, 'You're wasting your time, Eva. They're not seeing anybody!'

Oh *really*, I think. I love a good challenge. I've got this far and I'm not going to let anyone here stop me now. Imagine if I could get the boys to agree to a reading! That'd wipe the smiles off of some of these faces.

A door opens and everyone stops talking and waits

to see who will emerge. It is an official-looking man in his early thirties. Nathan and I know the Beatles have to be behind that door. Shoulders back, head held high, I start walking confidently towards him. He turns in my direction with a quizzical look in his eye and cocks his head to one side. 'What on earth does she think she's going to get from me?' says the look on his face. 'No interviews,' he snaps.

I'm sure he has said this sentence a hundred times in the last hour, so I look him straight in the eyes. 'I don't want to interview them. I've come to read the Beatles' hands. I'm Eva Petulengro; I'm expected. Would you let them know I'm here, please?'

I say these words not so much as a question, but as a command. His eyes narrow but I hold his gaze. To my amazement, he turns on his heels and shuts the door on me. Now my heart really is pounding. Where is Nathan? Suddenly I feel his camera bag dig into the small of my back.

'What did you say, gal?' he demands. 'You didn't blow it for us, did you?'

We wait for what seems like an eternity but must only be no more than two minutes. When the door starts to open, I take a step back. Had I done it? Had I talked my way into meeting the Fab Four?

To my amazement, four heads simultaneously, one on top of the other, appear round the door. Paul, John,

Ringo and George stare in my direction and look me up and down from top to toe, as an inquisitive dog might. As quickly as they appeared, they disappear and the door is firmly shut behind them. Bewildered, I wonder what will happen next. My heart is beating so hard in anticipation that it feels like it's about to jump out of my chest. The same man that had looked so surprised a few moments earlier now comes out of the door and says to me, very respectfully, 'Would you please follow me, Miss Petulengro'.

I turn my head and give a triumphant grin to the waiting reporters. 'Come along, Nathan,' I say and walk briskly towards the door. Nathan, hot on my heels, firmly shuts the door behind us.

We are shown into a small room which is normally used as some kind of an office and is filled with photos of the famous faces that have trodden the boards in the Hippodrome. One of the security men instantly eyes Nathan's camera bag. 'Sorry, mate. No cameras.' I open my mouth to speak, but before I can, he smiles and says, 'We have our own photographer.' I give a sigh of relief, as this is definitely a moment I want recorded for posterity!

George Harrison comes in first. He is bigger than I had imagined and puts me at ease straight away with his pleasant smile and down-to-earth manner. But what will his hand show? I can't wait to see.

George gestures for me to sit down and eagerly holds out his hands towards me. 'I've never had me hand read before. I've always been curious, though,' he exclaims. He raises an eyebrow and looks at me expectantly. He has very strong lines on his hands and I hear myself telling him that he will branch out into other things. The sensible side of me finds it difficult to believe that someone in the most famous band in the world would *not* stay doing this forever, but I will always tell a client what I see and not just what they want or expect to hear. His hands are well worn and I find him to be a soft and gentle man who speaks quietly and has great respect for what I do for a living. His interest in all things psychic seems to be a passion and I tell him this is something he should pursue. After half an hour, I complete my reading and we say our goodbyes.

Next through the door bounds a very lively Paul McCartney. Beaming and full of energy, he throws himself onto the seat and says, 'Come on then, what have you got to tell me?'

I think he is a little surprised when my reading reveals that Jane Asher, his girlfriend, will not be the one he marries. I tell him that he will meet someone from America and have a very good marriage to her. Someone very artistic and who does in fact share some of Jane's qualities. Both are fair in colouring, both are great cooks and independent in their careers. Suddenly there is a knock at the door. Paul calls out, 'I'm having my palm read, what do you want?'

'There's an urgent phone call for Eva,' says a young man. Immediately thinking that something is wrong with Mummy, I jump up, head for the door and walk quickly to the phone. 'Hello,' I say anxiously.

'It's me, I'm back.'

My heart jumps and I can feel a huge smile spreading across my face. It's my Johnnie. 'How did you know where I was?' I splutter.

'I got Pam to phone your home number and your mother told her you were backstage at the theatre.'

As I say my next words, I can't believe they are coming out of my mouth. 'Phone a taxi for me right now and send it to the back door of the theatre.'

My Johnnie is home at last and not even the Beatles are going to keep me away from him for another minute. I go back into the room and Paul is gone. After all, he did have a show to do!

Johnnie is the love of my life and for three years he has continually begged me to marry him. Each time, I said no. I was too scared to make that step, to marry a non-Romany against the wishes of my family. When he left Brighton five weeks ago, I really thought that this time I had lost him forever. We'd never been apart for such a long time and I had been missing him so much that something in me clicked – I finally realised he was all I'd ever wanted.

'John's back,' I say to Nathan. 'I'm leaving.'

The taxi arrives ten minutes later and I jump into it, not giving a second thought to the fact that I have left two of the most famous men of our time with unread hands. Years later, I'm glad that I didn't read John Lennon's palm and so did not foresee the tragic death that awaited him.

As I sit in the back of the taxi, which doesn't seem to be moving anywhere near fast enough, I run my fingers over the gold sovereigns on my bracelet and think of my grandmother, Alice Eva. She's such a strong woman: principled, far-sighted and brave. I've always looked up to her and my mother. If I say yes to Johnnie, if I marry someone from a non-Romany background, what will they think? Will they still be proud of me?

Do I dare take this step?

TWO

Mischief and Mayhem

The first memory I have is vividly imprinted in my mind. I was looking over the side of a pram, which was being pushed at speed across a field. It was very dark, but the sky was criss-crossed with search lights. There was a tremendous amount of noise as the anti-aircraft guns blazed away at the enemy planes overhead.

It was May 1941 and my mother and I were living in a field behind Weldon's car park in Spalding, Lincolnshire, where my father had arranged for us to stay before he left to join the army. There were around a dozen caravans occupied by gorger (non-Romany) people on the other side of the field from where we were parked. A short walk away was the Red Lion, a beautiful old inn in the marketplace, and it was behind there that my grandmother and the rest of the family had their wagons, or vardos, as we called them.

It had been raining and there was thick mud on the

ground as my mother struggled across the field, pushing the pram with me and her most precious belongings crammed into it. When she got to the gate, she found that it was locked. There was a high mesh fence all round the field because, in the summer months, it was used as a sports ground. Fairs were also held there and, during the winter, travelling people were allowed to stay on the site for a modest rent.

My mother picked me up, along with whatever else she could carry, and managed to climb over the high gate. Then she ran towards my grandmother's vardo, while bombs were dropping on the town and the guns were pounding away, spraying shrapnel everywhere.

We were almost there but some instinct told her not to try to complete her journey. She threw us both under the nearest caravan and we lay there, feeling the ground shudder from the bombs' impact.

Then it quietened. The planes went away and the sound of the guns receded. My mother found, just two inches away from my head, a lump of jagged metal, still red-hot, which would have sliced through my skull like butter. She kept that piece of shrapnel as a stark reminder of how precious life is.

Pulling me out into the open, Mummy picked me up again and made her way shakily to Granny's vardo. Shutters on the windows acted as blackout curtains, keeping any light from showing, but we could just make out Granny on her steps, peering out into the darkness, no doubt looking to see where the bombs might have fallen.

'Laura, is that you? Oh thank God,' she said. 'Get inside.'

The caravan was warm and cosy in the lamplight. I remember my muddy coat and shoes being stripped from my body and a warm blanket being tucked around me. After that, I must have fallen asleep.

Spalding is a quaint place, built along the River Welland. Running from the main high street were little narrow footpaths heading to the medieval priory. Little bits of history could be seen everywhere: the White Hart inn, opposite the Red Lion in the market square, was built in the fourteenth century and once housed Mary Queen of Scots, while the rest of the square was dominated by pretty Georgian buildings. But this lovely little country town, which had managed to survive hundreds of years untouched, had been badly damaged in a matter of minutes.

I assume Spalding had air-raid shelters, but none of my family would have gone into them. I don't know of any Romanies who ever used them – the fear of being enclosed, trapped underground, was too great. When the buzz bombs came along later in the war, I think our people believed they stood a sporting chance if they could run fast enough – foolish maybe, but this is the way the Romany mind works. We have always lived in open spaces and are used to our freedom. To be locked in and not be able to get out would feel like a death sentence to a Romany.

Obviously, out there in Lincolnshire, we were usually well away from the terrible bombings that the towns and cities had to put up with, but there was still plenty of evidence that the war was on. We were on one of the main flight paths to London and so we actually saw the Germans come and go on their bombing missions. One night, my mother's sister Vera came banging on the door. She rushed in saying, 'Bring Eva and come over to my vardo. There's a German who's bailed out of his plane and is on the loose.' As Mummy hesitated, Aunt Vera said, 'Come on, let's go! It's getting dark.'

My mother grabbed her big iron frying pan from the cupboard and swung it round her head. 'I'll be fine. If he tries to come into my vardo, he'll get more than he bargained for.'

'If you don't come with me, I'm staying here,' Aunt Vera said, sitting down and folding her arms.

'You can't leave your children, Vera. Don't be silly.'

In the end, my aunt won and we went back to her vardo for the night. I was put in bed with my cousins Daisy, who is my age, and her big sister Honour, who is three years older. Their father, my uncle Cardy (so called because as a boy he was 'quite a card'), sang to us to calm us down and get us to sleep. The lyrics went something like this: 'Toffee, chocolate, lollipops and ice cream . . .' and went on to list all the nice things to eat, including cakes, biscuits and strawberries.

Mummy was sharing Vera's bed, so Uncle Cardy went off to bed down with his brothers-in-law Nathan and Alger in their old vardo. We heard the next day that some men working in the fields had found the airman asleep under a hedge.

I was born in March 1939, so my memories of those early war years come in fragments. I do recall my baby brother Nathan being born in 1942 and named after my mother's father, Nathaniel. Before, Mummy had been able to leave me in the care of Shunty, her younger sister, who lived with Granny, but she would not leave a baby as young as Nathan. This meant that it was difficult for her to go out and work – she read palms and had a loyal circle of clients.

She was still able to dukker (palm-read) occasionally, though, as some of her clients would visit our vardo. There was one regular, a doctor's wife, who arranged to come along for a reading and to see the new baby. I was under strict instructions to behave myself and I had a new dress for the occasion, in pink Viyella with a matching smock. I knew I'd be placed on the steps of the vardo and told to stay there until

Mummy had finished attending to the client, under threat of dire punishment if I moved a step away. I couldn't stay still for more than a few minutes at a time and I knew it would feel like hours on those steps, so before the client arrived, I looked around the vardo for something to take with me to help the time pass. What I found was a pack of Craven A cigarettes and a box of matches, left behind by some relatives who had visited us the previous evening.

I remember finding it fascinating to watch grownups puffing away at those funny white sticks, blowing out clouds of smoke, or sometimes, magically, ring upon ring, reaching up to the roof of the vardo. It was something I had always wanted to try for myself and so I sneaked a cigarette out of the packet and secreted the box of matches. When the client arrived, I waited for Mummy to close the door to the vardo before tiptoeing quietly down the steps and sauntering innocently towards my secret hiding place under the grandstand, on the far side of the field.

There, crouched on my haunches, I surveyed the cigarette before placing it in my mouth, feeling incredibly grown up and sophisticated. I remember vividly how the taste of the cigarette soaked into my lips and I squirmed a little at the bitterness. I struck a match and lit it, drawing in with all of my breath, just as I had seen the grown-ups do. The smoke that I inhaled quickly made its way down the back of my throat like a furnace being lit. I not only choked, but spat everything out as a coughing fit overtook me. The red-hot ash fell into my lap, turning to orange and then grey. Watching in horror, I saw a hole begin to appear in my new dress. As soon as I managed to get my breath back, I crawled guiltily from my hiding place and ran back to the vardo, knowing that I would be in hot water if I was missing for too long. I stopped halfway back and looked down at my dress. There was not just one hole – the dress was covered in them. I wanted to run away, but where to?

'Eva!' I heard a voice call. My heart was in my mouth. If I didn't come, I knew I would be in trouble, yet I also knew I would be in deep trouble when she saw me. I started rubbing violently at the holes, which only seemed to make them more obvious. My eyes stung from the smoke and hot tears were now running down my face.

'Eva, come here now,' shouted Mummy. 'Where are you, child?'

Slowly putting one foot in front of the other, I started to walk towards the vardo. The steps that led up to it, right at this moment, seemed to be the steps of doom. When my mother saw me, bedraggled and mucky, she screamed in horror and pointed speechlessly at my dress.

That was the first time my mother spanked me, and it is a spanking I shall never forget. Maybe she was also relieved that I hadn't managed to set fire to myself in the process.

I was a feisty child, and a bloody nuisance. Unable to sit still for two minutes, I was always up to something and was very adventurous. One Christmas I almost learned how to perform on a trapeze. Some circus people had set up winter quarters near to us in Spalding and I used to watch them working out their new routines and practising.

I'd stare with horror at the fire-eaters, who'd douse cotton wool with methylated spirits, set fire to it, then put this flaming bundle in their mouths. Every time I saw it I was terrified they'd burn themselves – though of course they never did.

The trapeze artists were teaching their own children and, because I was always there watching, they taught me a few tricks too. Whether they were just being kind, I don't know, but they said that I was quite supple and doing very well. Suddenly I had visions of myself on the high wire, all beautifully made up and dressed in spangles, with the spotlight turned on me as all the other lights in the Big Top dimmed and the huge audience hushed while I tested the ropes before sailing into some death-defying triple somersault without a safety net. Actually, I never got more than about two feet above the ground, and then my mother found out where I had been disappearing to and that was the end of my ambition to become a circus performer!

My next escapade took place inside the vardo, where I was now kept in custody, since my mother dared not let me out of her sight. A chromium-plated screw from one of the cupboard doors had worked loose and, after I had fiddled with it for a while, it came away in my hand. To amuse myself, I balanced the flat head of the screw on the palm of my hand and then, having mastered that fairly simple operation, I thought I would find out how long I could balance it on the tip of my tongue.

I found out, and the answer was . . . not for long. I swallowed it! When I told my mother, she rushed me to the nearest hospital. This was one of those few occasions when Romanies would not rely upon their own remedies, but would call for a drabengro, or doctor. The drabengro at the hospital x-rayed me and showed the plate to my mother. Unfortunately, the screw was pointing downwards, which he said was dangerous because it could puncture something. I was put on a diet of thick, horrible porridge, with no liquids allowed at all, until the screw passed through me. It worked eventually, although I remember how cruel I thought my mother was being to me.

If it wasn't enough for my mother having to deal

with all my antics, there was the constant worry of another bomb attack, or – something that seemed even scarier at the time – the possibility of a gas attack. Thank God, it never did happen, but there were frequent scares. I do recall one particular occasion when my mother was absolutely terrified because we had no gas masks. The gorgers had all been issued with them through their town halls and schools, but when my mother applied, she was told that there were none left and she would have to wait until another supply came through. They advised her, while waiting and in case of a gas attack, to cover herself and the children with wet blankets. Consequently, whenever there was any rumour of a gas attack, the middle of the vardo was occupied by a bathtub full of water with three blankets soaking in it.

In the end, all these scares and dramas became too much for my mother, there on her own, and she decided she would move in with Granny.

THREE

Stick Fires and Happy Memories

My grandmother, Alice Eva, was a tiny woman, smart as a carrot, always beautifully groomed and dressed. She was very pretty and dainty when she was young and when I knew her she carried herself with the poise of a duchess.

Granny's wooden vardo was like a Wonderland to me, lit by two oil lamps with ruby-coloured glass shades which gave a soft, warm glow that made us feel so comfortable and cosy. We'd lie on the bed in the evening, our backs against goose-feather-filled pillows covered with large paisley shawls made from pure cashmere with fringes. I'd be drinking a cup of hot Horlicks and Granny would have a glass of barley wine. She would unpin her long, dark hair, which almost reached her waist, and I would brush it carefully with a silver brush until told to stop. When it was time for bed, Granny would turn on the radio and Vera Lynn and Benny Goodman would sing in the background while she told me stories about my grandfather and their children and I drifted off to sleep.

Alice Eva Taylor came from Hopton in Norfolk, where her family owned a lot of businesses and land. Like most Romanies, she met her future husband, Nathaniel Smith (or Petulengro in Romany), from time to time throughout their childhood at gatherings. She told me once that she fell in love with him at the age of eight and always knew she would marry him. They were roughly the same age, I believe.

Nathaniel, who was born in Gorleston, near Great Yarmouth on the Norfolk coast, in 1876, was a very independent young man with a great sense of humour. As a boy, his twinkling eyes made people think that he'd done something mischievous, or was about to, which is why he was nicknamed Naughty. His family were horse dealers, so he became one too, and he learned his trade from his father and uncles.

When he was about five, he ran into his father's vardo and said that Rajie, his favourite horse, was not well.

'What's the matter with him?' his father asked.

'I don't know, Daddy, but he is in pain.'

His father examined the animal and announced, 'This horse has colic.'

'I knew something was wrong; he's got the belly-ache!' Naughty said.

'It's something bad that he has eaten, so we will give him something to get rid of it,' his father said. After this, Naughty was known as 'the bellyache kid' for a while.

By the age of twenty, he was a very striking man, tall and well-built. He had style and grace, even though his arms seemed to go on forever; in fact, they hung below his kneecaps.

He had a natural sense of humour, as did Alice, and when they were together at gatherings everyone around could feel the magnetism between them. No one was surprised when, in true Romany fashion, the couple eloped, running away to nearby Thetford. On their return, Alice's mother gave her a gold charm bracelet, with five gold sovereigns hanging from it. It was traditional to pass on gold to daughters as a wedding present, for it was as good as money.

On the same day they returned to Hopton to receive the Romany blessing, their vardo was delivered. In preparation for his marriage, Nathaniel had secretly contacted Dunton's of Reading, a firm renowned for their beautiful vardos, which they had been making since 1880. He ordered for his bride a Reading wagon, known among Romanies as the Rolls-Royce of caravans.

Naughty selected each piece of wood that went into the building of the vardo, determined to have the best.

It was painted a rich ox-blood red on the outside with gold-leaf motifs. Steps led up to the footboard at the front of the caravan, where stood two water cans and a matching bowl for washing their hands and faces, made from alternating strips of brass and copper. To finish it off, there were two carriage lamps, also made of copper, one situated at each side of the door, to be lit in the evenings when they often sat outside by a stick fire and talked into the night about their future together.

Inside, he dictated the carvings and the design of the cut-glass mirrors in the doors which separated the beds (two doubles, on top of each other like bunk beds) from the living quarters. The mirrors were engraved with birds, bunches of grapes, vines and flowers, and the same design was artfully carved into the ceiling. Over the brass mantelpiece there was another splendid mirror, which reflected Alice's precious, delicate Dresden china ornaments. There were two oil lamps made of ruby cut-glass which bathed the whole caravan in a warm, relaxing glow. They also had the finest linen, china and silver. Granny's nine children were born in this caravan, as was I and many of my cousins.

Later, after their first three children were born, Naughty had a replica of the first vardo built. This one was painted in beautiful sage green, again with the gold leaf decoration. Eventually, as their brood grew, he ordered a third – he and Alice had one to themselves; the boys and girls took the other two. Each vardo had coloured leaded windows and stable doors. The horses that pulled the vardos were all heavy black-and-white cobs, trained by Naughty and standing at about fourteen hands high; there's no way less sturdy horses could have done that job. Generally, only one horse was used at a time, although two were needed to go up steep hills. That's probably why the family concentrated on travelling around flat parts of the country, like Norfolk and Lincolnshire. Naughty knew horses like the back of his hand and had a deep respect for the animal; his horses never travelled more than fifteen miles a day and were very well looked after. Famous racehorse owners would often seek out Naughty to get his advice and guidance on their own horses as he was so highly thought of within this circle.

Romanies did not believe in or even understand banks. It would have been hard in those days for them to use them anyway because of their travelling way of life. So Romanies put their money into gold and china. Both men and women would buy expensive gold necklaces, rings and sovereigns and wear them. They also often invested the money in diamond rings. Should money ever become tight, they would sell them, but wearing them seemed like the most obvious thing to do. This is why we see so many pictures of gypsies with gold-hooped earrings. Little did people know that this was them wearing their savings, so to speak.

Every Romany woman would proudly display the china of her or her family's choice. For the Petulengro family it was (and is) Crown Derby and this particular, very attractive design was handed down the family and bought by succeeding generations too.

The Romany lifestyle often seemed mysterious to gorger folk, who would sometimes attempt to make friends with Romanies with the sole purpose of trying to take a peek into a Romany vardo! But this is something Romanies never encouraged as, aware of their expensive ornaments, they were always afraid that word would get out and they would be a target for burglars.

Alice and Naughty were an incredibly happy couple and they fitted together perfectly. While he treated her like a princess, she managed to tame him and his wild ways. She was a woman who didn't suffer fools gladly and he respected her opinions. She also knew how to suppress his rebellious streak, something no one else had ever been able to do for him. He had always been mischievous by nature, hence his nickname, and would regularly tell his children stories that demonstrated how different a path his life could have taken when he was younger, thanks to his inability to do what he was told.

Naughty's brothers all claimed to be educated because they once went to school for five weeks. This was at Broome, in Norfolk, where the family had pulled in to paint the vardos. As usually happened when Romanies stopped somewhere for longer than a few days, the authorities insisted that while they were there, the boys would have to attend the village school. Having never been to school before, the other boys were curious about the experience and were quite happy to give it a try, but not Naughty. He wanted to stay at home and tend the horses, which he loved. Wild ones could not have dragged him to that school and, always the rebel, he never did go. He saw no reason why he should fit into the gorger way of life when he was a Romany.

I also remember being told a story of how he and his brothers were one day leaving a horse auction when they saw an old cart and horse in the street outside. They examined it and decided it was not worth bidding for. On the back of the cart there was a pile of sacks and, on top of these, an old worn-out pair of boots, obviously discarded by their owner and not in any condition to be worn by anyone.

Naughty picked up one of the boots and threw it to his brother, my great-uncle Olby, and, as high-spirited boys will, they had a general game of catch. All this, they didn't realise, was being observed by a policeman who, for want of something better to do, arrested them on a charge of stealing footwear – the rotten old pair of boots.

They had done nothing wrong; there had been no intention to steal anything. Though chastened by this end to their joke, it still seemed a bit of a lark and they had no doubt that this silly charge against them would be thrown out of court. When the brothers were asked what they had to say, they apologised in the manner they had been taught. All except Naughty, who looked at the magistrate as though he didn't think much of his intelligence for taking this stupid matter seriously and said, 'If I were going to steal, it would be something a lot more valuable than a worn-out pair of old boots, I assure you.' Luckily, all he got was a good telling off.

Like generations of his family before him, horses were in Naughty's blood and there was nothing anyone could tell him about a horse or its fitness. He knew all the tricks of the trade and could spot a cheat immediately, but he was also known for his honesty and would never have used his knowledge to cheat anyone himself. Later, during the First World War, he supplied horses to the cavalry.

The profit they earned from their horse trading was sometimes counted in shillings rather than pounds, but this was neither here nor there to Naughty and his brothers. The Romany never counted his time; he was a free man and rejected the idea of a regular job and steady wages as that would have taken away some of that freedom. So whatever Naughty earned was profit and, in that way, he always got the best of the bargain.

He would also tend horses and was a blacksmith, again something his father and his father before him had done. As Naughty learned from his father, so he would go on to teach his sons. He expected that their future livelihoods would depend on their ability to deal knowledgeably in horses.

Naughty and Alice Eva's first child, Nathan, was born around 1902 by my estimate. He was a talented boy who, had he been educated, would have most likely become a writer. He had a real gift for description and could hold the attention of the most impatient audience with his fascinating tales and insight into life.

He was the first of what was to be a brood of nine, all born roughly eighteen months to two years apart, as best I can tell. Alger came next and was the most animated of the brothers. He was a wonderful tap dancer, as was his father, although his shy nature when among outsiders prevented him from being the showman he could have been.

Cissie was the oldest of Alice's girls and was said to be the most beautiful. Elders in the family often said she reminded them of Merle Oberon, the famous actress who would star in *Wuthering Heights* with Laurence Olivier. She had a faraway look in her eyes, as if she were gazing at something only she could see. Cissie had very thick, naturally black, curly hair, as did all of Alice's five daughters. Cissie's framed her angelic face and lovely tanned skin. But what made her all the more beautiful was her character.

A representative of an advertising company for a chocolate firm once approached the family and said that they would be very interested in having Cissie on the front of one of their chocolate boxes, as she had been spotted by one of the directors. Naughty went mad and refused in no uncertain terms. Shortly after that, a famous artist asked to paint Cissie when he saw her. He approached Alice and, although she knew Naughty wouldn't approve, she couldn't resist eventually agreeing. So, behind his back, she arranged for the artist to visit the stopping ground on the days when she knew her husband and their sons would be out tending farmers' horses. She made sure that she and all her sisters were present as chaperones. I've heard that the painting was amazingly stunning, but the artist kept it, of course, and the family has never been able to track it down.

If this makes Naughty sound like a strict parent, well, he was, but not as strict as Alice who, with so many children to look after, had to let them know who was in control. One glance from her was enough to make the culprit of a misdemeanour own up, or make one of the children finish a job they should have done but hadn't. But Granny told me once that although she and Naughty would put on a stern face at some of the children's antics, they would often go into the vardo, out of sight, and laugh until they both cried. Granny used to say that the reason she and my grandfather had such a wonderful relationship was because they had laughed together since they were children.

Their third son, Walter, was a shy boy who never liked to leave his father's side. Walter and his father could not have looked more different, yet they fitted together like two peas in a pod and were always very close.

Lena came next. Tall and willowy, she had a husky voice and seemed to always be laughing. She was followed by Adeline in 1912 (a date easy to remember as it was the same year the *Titanic* sank), who looked very much like her sisters, but had the most amazing eyes, a stunning green-brown that seemed to change colour every time you looked at her. She was a feisty girl, dominant in her opinions and quite haughty. Everyone in the family used to laugh about how obvious it was that she would grow into a woman who could take care of herself.

Laura Eva, my mother, was born around 1914 – another year easily remembered, coinciding as it did with the outbreak of the First World War. She only spoke when she had something to say, but her family would always stop what they were doing whenever they saw she was about to speak. She had a sense of humour that would make a cat laugh. My mother was the gentlest soul I've ever known, with the most wonderful glass-half-full outlook on life. Petite and pretty, she could easily have stepped off the pages of a beauty magazine.

Vera came next, shorter than her sisters and curvier, almost cherub-like in comparison to their skinny frames. She had big, round eyes with lashes that swept her cheeks. She insisted on looking different from the other girls and, as a teenager, begged for her long, curly hair to be cut into a bob. With the curls refusing to be tamed, this simply led to her looking more jolly than sophisticated.

The final girl, Shunty, was a late child, probably born in 1928. Although she was warm-hearted and kind most of the time, she was no pushover either and could be sharp-tongued when the occasion demanded it.

As the girls grew older, they would often debate about their ages. The conversation would be repeated again and again by my aunts over the years and it went like this: Vera would say to my mother, 'Now, I'm eighteen months younger than you.' My mother would say to Vera, 'Well, Adeline is two years older than me, so how old is Cissie?' And so it would go on. Never having had birth certificates (Romany babies were more often than not delivered by female family members), there was no official record they could refer to. Whereas nowadays women often lie about their age and start counting backwards from the age of about thirty-five, my aunts really weren't sure how old they actually were, but found this more funny than distressing.

A family of eleven makes for overcrowding, especially for someone like Alice who liked to keep her homes spotless. So when they had stopped somewhere, Naughty would make rod tents, known as benders. In appearance they're not unlike igloos. The supports are made from fine, young, supple willow which has been soaked overnight to make it more flexible and is then bent to shape and allowed to season. These tents were quite simple for Naughty to dismantle and reassemble. The covering was a waterproof woven material, ordered specially from a large mill, held together by sharpened hawthorn pins. Four people could sleep easily in each vardo, but when there were more, a bender would be used.

Tarpaulin covered the floor of the tent, which was then topped by a huge Persian carpet. During the day the tent served as a big dining room, and in the middle would be a table covered with the most beautiful starched, white lace tablecloths. In the winter, when the weather was too fierce to build a fire outside, Naughty and his sons would build a fire inside the tent, the smoke escaping from a hole in the top and spiralling into the cold night air. The family would sit around the fire and talk and eat, and after dinner they would sing and play their instruments. Alice was a gifted musician on the violin and accordion, and all the children had their own special instruments. Naughty would also lay down his bench, a trestle table with fold-down legs, on top of which he would teach the children new tap steps. The bench would also be used as a table for preparing food on outside the vardo.

Alice always said that her husband reminded her of Dan Leno, a famous music-hall clog-dancer in the late nineteenth century, and this was never truer than when he was tapping away on his boards for her. It's a saying in our family that it would have broken Dan Leno's heart if he ever saw Naughty dance as my grandfather was so much better than him!

The tent was also used by the children when it was too cold to play outside, and at night it was turned into a bedroom and used for extra sleeping space. Even with snow thick on the ground, they were the snuggest and warmest of children in that bender tent.

I have photographs of some of my aunts and uncles as teens, posing outside the bender tent in the 1920s. They had caught the eye of a photographer, who took numerous pictures of them dressed in their best clothes. When I heard my family talking about him, I asked what his name was. 'Old Tit' was the reply, with much laughter. He had a slight speech impediment, so when he was ready to take his picture and would command them to 'Hold it!' it always came out as 'Old Tit'.

When spring came, the family would travel around Norfolk and Lincolnshire, wherever their fancy took them. Since the end of the First World War, there were more and more cars on the roads, and the roads themselves were gradually being tarmacked by the Irish who were coming over to work in England at that time. For the Romany, it made it harder to leave a 'pukkering cosh', a clod or a bunch of sticks used as a sign. In the old days, when a group of Romanies were all heading in the same direction and some were leaving later than others, it was always agreed that when coming to a fork in the road, those who knew the route best would pull a big clod of earth from the side of the road and throw it into the middle of the lane that they were going to take. Now that cars were taking over the roads, it was not possible to leave a clear signal for fellow travellers to follow. It was a small thing, but perhaps the first sign that their heritage was being taken away from them.

Naughty obviously never thought the Romany way of life would change. His mind could not grasp the idea that caravans would soon no longer need horses to pull them – that this job would be done by motorcars. Cars were a gorger means of transport. Romanies lived under the stars and their horses were a central part of their lives. Romanies travelled where their whims led them. They were no part of the gorger society; they took nothing from it and asked nothing of it, except perhaps tolerance, the right to live their lives the way Romanies had done for centuries.

This was always Naughty's philosophy. But how could he know that the time would come when his bright canopy of stars would be rolled up like the backcloth of a travelling show, that the costumes and the scenery would all be packed away, that the play would be over? It would not be long before the traditional Romany way of life, the only life Naughty and Alice Eva had ever known, would change beyond all recognition.

But in 1920 they weren't worried about this. They were able to travel without being harassed. In fact, when they arrived in a new town, people were actually pleased to see them and many of the farmers and their families looked forward to the seasons when they knew they might return. They knew Naughty was skilled at treating their animals, horses especially, and Alice had many herbal remedies for their ailments. More than that, Alice had a gift for clairvoyance.

FOUR

First Up, Best Dressed

'My husband is having an affair,' the woman blurted out, before Alice could even start her reading.

'Are you sure?' Alice asked gently.

'He doesn't spend any time with me and when he does come home he smells of another woman's perfume. The other day, I even found lipstick on his collar as I was washing one of his shirts.'

Alice didn't have to be a clairvoyant to know that this was someone who clearly wasn't loved and probably never had been. The man in question had married her to do his housework, no more, no less. Just by looking around, she could see the woman kept a marvellous house, very clean and tidy, but there was no feeling of love there.

'This isn't his first affair though, is it?' she asked.

'No,' the woman admitted, tears falling from her eyes and hitting her apron.

'Here's what I want you to do,' began Alice. 'I want

you to pack up his shirts and give them to him. Tell him that his fancy woman can wash his shirts from now on. You run a perfect house and you have a lot to give someone who will love you back. You have good family.'

'Yes, I do,' she replied, 'but I haven't seen them in a long time.'

'They will comfort you,' Alice said. 'Oh, and don't forget to put his smalls in the package too!' she added with a smile and a twinkle in her eye. With this, the woman started giggling and the tears began to dry.

My aunt Cissie, who was about fourteen at the time, was sitting quietly during the reading. Alice would often take her to visit clients who were not too far away. The time the two spent travelling together in Alice's smart pony and trap was very precious to them. On this particular day, Cissie realised that not all relationships were as full of love and support as her parents'. It also opened up her eyes to the fact that her mother was not as closed a book as she may have seemed. With her mother's upbeat view of life and her knack of making people laugh, she could help even when a person had particularly unhappy problems to deal with.

Alice was training Cissie in palm-reading and clairvoyance, as she would go on to do with all her daughters. This was very traditional in Romany families, where the men would work with horses and the women would read people's hands. People often wonder why Romanies have a special gift for clairvoyance and I believe it is because our race is taught from birth to say how we feel and to keep an open mind. We didn't go to school and were not taught to place limitations on ourselves. Granny used to say that gorgers had their heads filled with world affairs, history, geography and so on at school, but Romanies had room in their brains to allow their natural instincts to develop. We all have these instincts – how many times have you picked the phone up before it rang, made extra food and had someone unexpectedly turn up for dinner, or told yourself 'I knew that would happen'? The gift of being able to predict the future of others is something that has run in our bloodline for centuries. Girls as young as five and six would be taught to recognise the meaning of the lines on a person's hands and as they got older they were taught how to interpret them.

Alice was a skilled clairvoyant with many regular clients, from farmers' wives to royalty. One of her most treasured possessions was a crystal ball presented to her by Princess Marie Louise, one of Queen Victoria's granddaughters, which I inherited eventually. When, many years later, I was invited to read hands at a ball thrown by Prince Edward at the Grosvenor House Hotel in London in 1987 and was asked if I could donate anything to the charity auction, I gave them the crystal ball – since it came from royalty and the auction was on behalf of royalty, I felt Granny wouldn't mind. It was Andrew Lloyd Webber, the composer, who bid for and won it.

Each year when the family travelled, they would stop on the outskirts of Wainfleet, a pretty market town five miles inland from Skegness in Lincolnshire. The town was (and is) known for its famous Batemans beers and ales, which Naughty always made the most of. In fact, he was such a familiar sight at the pub that the black mongrel who lived there would often follow him home at night. Alice would laugh that he was making sure Naughty got home all right. Who knows, perhaps she was right!

During their stay, a big chauffeur-driven car would be sent to take Alice to Petwood House, the home of Sir Archibald and Lady Weigall. One year Alice was invited to attend a garden tea party at Petwood and the girls were particularly excited, as they knew their mother would receive large tips and a promise of glamorous clothes from the ladies attending. These ladies and their children only wore an outfit once or twice, and my mother and aunts knew that in a few days' time they'd be very well dressed in expensive cast-offs. 'First up, best dressed,' as Alice would say to them when they argued about who got to wear what.

When the day of the party came, Alice dressed herself in all her finery and waited by the roadside for the grand car to arrive and take her to the even grander house. She knew she'd be smuggled into the party by the back entrance, but this didn't bother her. When she arrived she was taken to a back room, where she immediately began a long day of work as the ladies attending all took it in turns to go and see her. It was all very hush hush and the men were unaware that their wives and daughters were visiting this Romany clairvoyant and palmist in a back room of the splendid house. Nor, Alice thought to herself, did they know that some of their children were not their true next of kin but conceived by some misadventure, and nor were these men aware that some of their wives did not love them but had married them simply to be free of their parents or to get out of debt. Alice would keep these secrets; she always did, of course. But she told me once that it made her wonder how so many people could live a life that didn't truly make them happy. Sure, she and Naughty had hard times, many of them. But she wouldn't change what she had for all the tea in China.

That evening there was a commotion amongst the dogs and horses outside the vardos. 'Who's there?' shouted Naughty. As quick as a flash, he was up on his feet. It was Alice's pony that was making the biggest fuss, bucking all over the place. Afraid that he might damage her trap, Naughty headed towards the pony, rolling up his sleeves. He listened for the noise that had disturbed the animals. Naughty was always ready for the unexpected and never afraid of anyone or anything. As the purr of a car in the distance grew louder, followed by the beeping of a horn, Naughty relaxed and Alice's face lit up.

'Girls,' she beamed. 'Stand up and make yourselves look presentable. It's clothes time.'

The driver of the car stepped out. 'Hello, Mrs Petulengro, how are you?'

'Joseph,' Alice said. 'How's that lovely wife of yours keeping?' Joseph was Sir Archibald and Lady Weigall's chauffeur and he and Alice had known each other for years now. Joseph walked round to the back of the car and, with a deft flick of his finger, opened the boot. The girls rushed round and saw several bags, which they couldn't wait to get their hands on. Grabbing the bags and taking them into the vardo, they couldn't stop giggling with excitement. They immediately opened the bags and stroked the fabrics – silks, satins and pure wool – as one would a newborn baby. One bag contained hats and shoes, some adult clothes and also, to the girls' delight, some children's clothes and two beautiful lace tablecloths. Tonight they would be dining well and dressing well!

Alice always made sure her children were well

dressed, at least when they left the vardo. One day Mummy and Vera were walking down a lane on their way to the birthday party of a farmer's child, a family they had known for years. They were both wearing beautiful white dresses given to them by a doctor's wife who used to pass all her children's clothes to them. They came to two black poles in the lane and Vera ran to one, deciding to swing around it. What she didn't realise was that the poles had just been painted and suddenly Vera's hands, her legs and her beautiful white dress were all covered in thick black paint. Picturing her horrified face many years later, Granny would still cry with laughter.

When the vardos were rested at night on the verges of the country lanes through which they travelled, Naughty would build a fire outside and then push a stake into the ground, which would hold an iron stew pot. Alice would cook delicious recipes handed down through the generations, flavoured with fresh herbs picked from the fields.

Naughty had three greyhounds, two lurchers and a little terrier, which were useful for following a rabbit or hare down a hole and bringing it out. Although many people choose to course for fun, for Naughty and the rest of my family it was the only way to put food on the table. People often think it's awful that we hunt our own meat. We, on the other hand, find it far more comforting to know that the animal was killed as quickly and humanely as possible. When hunting, the men would rely on their instincts – a kind of clairvoyance, if you like – to know in which direction to go to find food.

Many of the dishes that Alice prepared were the same as those prepared and eaten by gorgers, but they also ate Romany-style. They often dined on freshly picked mushrooms, which tasted unbelievably good. Moorhen, partridge and wild duck were all regularly on the menu. Pheasants are in season around Christmas time and one of Alice's favourite recipes was to quarter an apple and put it inside the bird, then squeeze half a lemon over the breast. On top of that went some bacon and then Alice would line a dish with bread and place the bird onto it. While it was cooking, the juices from the bird would soak into the bread and, together with the fat from the bacon, it made it a dish fit to set before a king.

There is another dish called Joey Grey which was a family favourite. Joey Grey, a traveller who lived many years before my grandparents, is supposed to have concocted it when he fell on hard times. Funny to think, then, that years later we all considered it a real treat. Alice would fry onions, to which water and salt and pepper would be added. She would then throw some sliced potatoes into the frying pan, until the water was just covering them, and simmer them until the potatoes were cooked. A gravy flavouring would then be added and, when it was ready, thick bread and butter would be dipped into it. Delicious and warming, it would set them up ready for a hard day's toil. Today, most Romany families make it with Oxo and Bisto and may add some steak or sausage to give the meal more substance. I don't think old Joey Grey ever realised how famous he would become for his pauper's dish and that people would go on to enjoy the meal which was named after him even into the twenty-first century.

My family would also pick nettles to make tea (which was meant to be good for the liver) and the men would make beer from them, using the nettle tops. I never drank it as I was growing up, but I've been told that it tastes remarkably like Champagne!

When the boys were not around, Mummy and her sisters would apply Fuller's earth, mixed into a paste with some lemon juice and water, to their skin as a face pack. They would clean the skin with witch hazel and apply the paste, leaving it on until it dried like mud, and then use witch hazel again to clean it off.

For their hair, they would use a couple of ounces of rosemary spikes, a couple of ounces of a herb called southernwood, the same of red sage and an ounce of bay leaves, all soaked in boiling water and mixed together. The water was then massaged into the scalp morning and night for thick, full hair.

All these treatments were passed down through the generations, and continue to be now, and I remember one particularly unusual one for warts. They would steal a bit of meat from the Sunday joint and rub it on the wart, after which they would bury the meat in the ground. The idea was that as the meat rotted, the wart would drop off. I've got no idea how this works, but I can assure you it does!

Romanies have always been known for their ability to cure all ills using concoctions made only from what nature has to offer, and through the ages gorgers have turned to us for help with curing all sorts of problems. But one evening when Naughty was in the pub and had been getting sick of the locals asking him for advice for their ailments when he just wanted to have a relaxing drink after a long day on the road, one of the regulars approached him, complaining about his problem with baldness.

'I'll tell you the real secret to growing your hair back,' Naughty said with a wry smile. 'Fresh cow dung, strained off. Why don't you get some for yourself and rub it into your hair every morning?'

With this, Naughty downed the rest of his drink, turned on his heels and walked back to his vardo to try to find a bit of peace and quiet. He didn't think much about the incident and didn't have a chance to go back to the pub until three months later, when the family returned from more travels.

He decided to give the public house another try and, to his annoyance, the same man came up to him again, only this time he looked slightly different.

'Do you mind if I join you?' he said. 'I just wanted to thank you. My wife, especially.'

On closer inspection, Naughty realised that this man actually had a new growth of hair on the top of his head. 'Er, you're welcome,' Naughty said. He laughed all the way back to the vardo, whereupon he told Alice the story.

Alice was in stitches. 'Well, manure does make things grow, doesn't it, Naughty? All sorts of things by the sound of it!' Granny told me that they were still laughing about it days later.

FIVE

Life is a Roller coaster

It was early 1927 and the family were on their way from Sleaford to Woodhall Spa, a village between Lincoln and Skegness near to the home of Sir Archibald and Lady Weigall, when they had an encounter that would change their lives.

A car came towards them from the other direction and pulled up at the side of the lane, about a hundred yards in front of them. A young man jumped out of the car and waved, having recognised the wagons. The family pulled the vardos into a handy field entrance.

'Naughty,' the man said. 'Good to see you again. I've been hoping I'd run into you.' The two men clasped each other's hands with a firm shake and patted each other on the back.

'Get some tea on, girls,' Naughty shouted. They sat down together on the verge while Nathan and Alger set about making up a fire.

'It must be fate that I've run into you, Naughty,'

the man said. 'I'm building an amusement park in these parts, which would be perfect for Alice and the girls to set up business at.'

'What, settle down in one place?' asked Naughty.

'It's only for six months of the year, and I have a feeling my new venture is really going to take off,' retorted the young man.

'Where is this place anyway?' asked Naughty.

'It's in Skegness, and I'm hoping you'll predict it will be a great success,' he replied with a smile. 'I'm off to London now to tie up a few loose ends, but I'll be back in Skeggy in a day or so. Come and have a look and see what you think.' Without waiting for his tea, he jumped back in his car and drove off.

'It can't do any harm, I suppose, just to have a look,' Alice said, with curiosity in her voice. 'He's always been ambitious and a hard worker. I'm sure it'll be an adventure to see the amusement park, if nothing else.' Despite her words, at that moment in time, Alice had a gut feeling that it would be more than a little interesting to her and her family.

The young man's name was Billy Butlin.

Billy was the son of Bertha Hill, who was from a very well-known and respected fairground travelling family. The Hills, Butlins and Petulengros had known each other for years and were good friends.

Although not well educated, young Billy had a sharp

business instinct. Having worked for a couple of years at the Hills Travelling Fair, he saw that there was money to be made in setting up his own amusement park in Skegness. Ordinary people were getting annual holidays now and choosing to go to the seaside, only to be kicked out of their bed and breakfast accommodation every morning. He knew that if he could keep them entertained in his park, they would spend their money with him, rather than with the other traders. He'd leased some land from the Earl of Scarborough and, as well as the usual attractions like the roller coaster, was looking for novelties and thought Alice's palm-reading would offer something different. In any event, the family had some beautiful daughters and Billy was a sucker for a pretty face, as are most men.

When Billy suggested to Alice that she open a palmistry booth, Alice felt it was an answer to her prayers. A six-month season without travelling. No more knocking on strangers' doors, but letting the people come to you instead. Recently, Alice and Naughty had been starting to find that they were not as welcomed by strangers as they had been and, as a result, money was harder to make. They didn't want to see their children left behind by the times, unable to make a living. All of the children were teenagers by now apart from Shunty, who was not yet born, and for the first time in their lives the Petulengro young men and women would be mixing with non-Romany people.

The family knew Mr Henshall, who owned the Royal Oak public house in the village of Ingoldmells near Skegness, a stone's throw from the amusement park, behind which he had a caravan site. He agreed to rent it to them for the season, which lasted from Easter to after the August bank holiday.

The month they had to wait for the park to open seemed like a year. The night before opening day, they were all full of anticipation. The girls were planning what they would wear and doing their beauty preparations and they hardly slept a wink.

The big day arrived. Adeline had bought new court shoes, but found they pinched her toes, so Lena suggested she poured boiling water into them, left them for five minutes and then put them on the wrong feet, which was common practice for stretching suede or leather. She breathed a sigh of relief when she tried them on and they fitted better so she wouldn't have to worry about not being able to walk all day!

Just inside the park was a roller coaster and underneath it, at street level, was a little parade of sites, created to look like caves hewn out of the rocky face of a cliff, but actually made from plaster. Alice's first booth at Skegness was one of these caves. There was a brightly coloured velvet curtain just inside the mouth of the cave, its wide hem filled with sand to weigh it down and stop the sea breeze blowing it up and revealing who was inside. Once through the curtain, the inside was a kind of dome with uneven walls, which had the exact appearance of damp rock. Alice also took another site at the other end of the amusement park and planned to run the businesses with her daughters.

Alice had ordered signs for the palmistry places, which were to be fixed outside on the walls. When they arrived at the site, she was horrified, for the signs read: 'Madam Eva, Romany Palmist and Clairvoyant. Patronised by Royalty'. Glaringly, the name Petulengro was omitted. Apparently, the sign writer didn't know how to spell it! Thereafter, she was known as Madam Eva all over Lincolnshire.

Soon queues began to form outside both the palmistry places. It cost two and sixpence to have one hand read and five shillings for both, so the money began to flood in.

Alice had taught her daughters how to greet and speak to the clients, how not to let the clients tell them anything and to keep them quiet while the reading was in progress. When clients did not have anything interesting in their hands, or had short lifelines, the girls would watch as their mother expertly found something positive to say. We are there, after all, to make the client feel safe and secure about their future, not petrified of it. Sometimes we play the role of coun-sellor, sometimes of priest. Many of our clients see us as a friend, but one they can tell their secrets to, unlike their real friends, who they're frightened will judge them. The eldest girls, Cissie, Lena and Adeline, were the first of the sisters to start giving readings on their own at the park, while Mummy and Vera continued to watch and learn the trade.

There were other travelling people who had conces-sions in the park too, and as the girls stood by the door of the palmistry place, lots of young men would naturally hang around and try to chat them up. Their brothers would do shifts, making sure that no one looked at their sisters in the wrong way – and that their sisters weren't eyeing up the boys either! Such behaviour was definitely a no-no.

The boys were also busy earning a living taking photographs, having bought two Aptus cameras, one of the first instant cameras. Set on tripods, they took sepia photographs which developed in only two to three minutes. Alger and Nathan kept themselves busy doing this and charged a shilling a picture.

I'm sure that being attractive young men definitely helped when it came to persuading the women to have their photographs taken. Nathan, the eldest, was tall and debonair, with a slightly quizzical grin, and was often likened to the actor Rudolph Valentino. Alger looked similar to Nathan and many would say not dissimilar to Ronald Coleman, although not quite as tall. Twinkling eyes gave the impression to those he met that he was keeping some sort of a secret. He was as opinionated as his sister Adeline, but they never had an argument. Disagreements and banter, yes, but no big fall-outs. Now that he was older, he often joined his father in the public house and had already earned himself the nickname 'the Fish' because he could drink so much and could actually hold it. This was not something his mother was proud of, however.

Walter, who was by now about fifteen, was a quiet lad who had inherited a more respectable nickname: Lavengro, which means scholar. He was noted for his good use of herbs and, along with his father, was always in demand by local farmers to tend to their sick horses. An animal will often know which herb or plant to eat to make itself better if it has bellyache and Walter also seemed to know what would work, even when the best vet in town had given up.

The atmosphere in the park was frenetic and it was an incredibly noisy place, with the carousel blasting out 'Blaze Away' and popular tunes of the day, which were all fast-paced in order to add to the excitement. The barkers on the stalls would yell out, 'Win a lovely coconut! Throw a double top to win a tanner!' The excited screams from children and the people on the roller coaster and the waltzer, together with the smell of hot dogs and candy floss, added to the unforgettable atmosphere. My family would always talk about the pure exhilaration they felt simply walking from stall to stall. It was an incredibly exciting place to be.

The shops of Skegness also held great joy for the girls, who now had money in their pockets. They could pick out and buy their own clothes and would often buy material to make copies of dresses and suits they had seen on their frequent trips to the movies. They would use Vaseline on their eyelids, mixed with a tiny bit of soot from the fire in the vardo. This resulted in a glossy shadow which made their eyes look enormous. A little lipstick, topped with Vaseline, made their lips glossy and would also be used as rouge for their cheeks. This was all done out of the sight of the boys or their father, who would never have approved.

Throughout that first summer, the girls, all of whom were undeniably beautiful, were attracting many admirers. Alice had instructed them not to encourage the attentions of the gorger boys. 'Do not make eye contact. If someone is looking at you, look the other way!' she said. 'If you give a man any encouragement, you'll never get rid of him.'

The brothers had made friends with some of the boys who worked in the amusement park and other traders, and they were full of news about the dance hall and the live band music played there. Much as they and their sisters longed to go, they were wary of approaching their parents about it, fearing that they would never approve. They weren't supposed to talk to the gorgers, let alone dance with them! Adeline and Nathan plotted together over how best to persuade their parents, deciding to say they didn't need to dance with the gorgers as they had each other.

Much to their surprise, when they did approach their parents, Naughty and Alice gave their permission, albeit with some very strong dos and don'ts. The girls all loved dancing because it was in their Romany blood, but that's all they were given parental consent for: to dance – with their brothers. They were not to start chatting with gorger boys and they were certainly not allowed to date them. The horror of the idea was sufficient for dire warnings to be unnecessary. The girls were to be shadowed closely by their minders/brothers. They were never told whether the boys got the same instructions about gorger girls, but there wasn't much they could do anyway, with four attractive sisters in their care.

When the time came to attend the first dance, they could not believe the difference between live music and the recorded kind. They danced to songs such as 'Who's Sorry Now?', 'Somebody Loves Me' and 'You're the

Cream in My Coffee'. The evening went so very quickly and soon they were on their way home, making plans for their next visit with great anticipation. Freedom at last! At least, it was to them.

The gorger boys must have been puzzled, to say the least, by the girls' initial consistent refusals of all offers. But on later visits the girls did not always refuse and their brothers would prop up the bar and enjoy a few drinks, keeping their own company, which suited them just fine. Besides, they did sometimes manage a dance with the gorger girls. They had an agreement – we won't tell if you don't.

It never went further than a dance, though, even if once or twice the girls tried to escape their chaperones. Even in those considerably less permissive days, a boy would have felt uncomfortable at the idea of having a big brother breathing down his neck while walking a girl home. Their companions were always warned off with the threat of grim retribution in the event of any romantic attachment. The would-be Romeos were undoubtedly left discouraged.

And so it went on throughout that summer. When the season drew to a close, there were some heavy hearts on board the vardos as they left Skegness behind them. They compensated for it by reassuring each other that in six months they would return to the hustle and bustle that they had enjoyed. With a taste for their new-found freedom, it was going to seem like a long six months.

Alice realised that with this new way of life, travelling less, it would be sensible to buy a plot of land that her family and other Romany people who visited them could pull onto. Not far from Skegness was another of their usual stopping grounds, the Lamb and Flag in the village of Whaplode, and near to the pub was an old bakery which was up for sale. Alice, who was very religious, thought this was a gift from God. She had always been a canny old bird who saved, not squandered, what she earned, so she promptly made a deal and bought it.

She also realised something else: the wagons were cumbersome and bender tents were now a thing of the past, while there were all kinds of new vardos that gorger people were taking to which were pulled by cars and not horses. When she brought up the idea of switching to this new mode of transport, the boys were quite excited, as travelling wouldn't take as long and it's every boy's dream to own a car. Alice made arrangements for all of the boys to have driving lessons and, as they knew a lot of people in Whaplode, some of whom already had cars, there was no problem when it came to practising.

She bought three modern aluminium caravans: one for the boys, one for the older girls and one for her and Naughty, but also kept the Romany Reading vardos, which meant so much to them all, as permanent quarters on the old bakery site.

So they had finally made some roots for their family, for the very first time in their long history. It was both scary and exciting; so many aspects of their way of life seemed to be changing, and they all wondered what further changes were waiting round the corner for them.

SIX

Talent Shows and Wedding Bells

'No Gypsies' was a sign the family were starting to see more and more in pub yards, where traditionally travellers would have been allowed to stay. The 1930s was a time of tension in the country and it was no longer safe to turn up at a place where some people may not know you. The industrial areas of Britain had already been through a recession in the 20s, but Lincolnshire was agricultural land, growing flowers and vegetables that were delivered all over the country. It wasn't the first county to be hit by problems, but it couldn't escape forever. Things became worse after the Wall Street Crash of 1929 led to the Great Depression. In Britain the effects lasted until at least 1933, with long dole queues in some parts of the country. Many people were literally begging for food. Suddenly, the Romany way of life began to look more and more appealing, for they were free and independent, and many gorgers around this time decided that they too would take to the road. Many came down from the Welsh hills, desperate to find a way of surviving. They would go from door to door selling things, begging and pretending to read hands.

For these gorgers, living on the road was not as easy or romantic as they had expected. Some of these people degenerated into thieves and con artists, owed rent to farmers and spoiled the countryside, leaving litter and rubbish at the stopping places. Not all of them, but some of them. It only took a few to spoil things for the real Romanies, though, as people were unable, or unwilling maybe, to distinguish between Romanies and other gypsies, including their own gorger kind. Many people decided that we were all 'dirty gypsies'.

Some of these new travellers would get drunk and start fights in pubs, so landlords became wary of allowing travellers to pull in to their yards and, of course, the residents of the towns and villages became more cautious. Farmers no longer welcomed them due to the bad state non-Romanies were now leaving their land in. 'Hedge crawlers' and 'dirty gypos' were phrases heard more and more often.

The old romantic idea of the gypsy was dying fast. Scrap metal had become a gypsy trade by this time and their stopping grounds often looked more like salvage yards. This all contributed to the notion of gypsies being dirty and anti-social, and the resentment people felt very quickly began to turn to hatred.

Naughty and Alice became more and more concerned by this growing hostility. By 1933 they had a teenage family, as well as Shunty, who was five, and they did not want their children, at an impressionable age, to be unduly affected by it. This, I am sure, was the reason for the change in their way of life. They must have known then that their children would never live in the traditional Romany way, as their parents and grandparents had done, and that it was time for them to start making changes.

Alice and Naughty now had a wintering place to stay. The vardos towed by horses would draw in for the winter months at Spalding. Although Alice still owned the bakery site at Whaplode, she allowed other travellers to pull onto it, as it was a little bit out in the sticks and Spalding was rather like their home town to them. Travelling was impossible in the winter months because of the weather. Money was short and life was hard.

The family stayed in a field behind the eighteenth-century Red Lion pub and hotel in Spalding's marketplace. Fairground and circus families would also stay for the winter in nearby Weldon's car park, and they would all swap stories about some of the less reputable characters taking to the roads. One of Granny's favourites was the story of a family of confidence tricksters. This story went round all the travelling communities, but nobody we met had actually encountered them. It goes like this.

The story was about a man called Thomas, his wife Becky and their beautiful daughter Diana. It is said that the couple were once in the theatre, but came to put their acting talent to a less reputable use. Apparently, they could only visit a place once, never to return, although they earned a very good living in return for paying this price.

They would call in to a new town or village, where-upon Becky would go to all the shops, obtain credit by false pretences and leave with food, clothes, anything she could get. This was her job, so to speak. Meanwhile, Thomas would advertise in the local paper to sell their wagon. When prospective buyers came to look at it, he would offer it at a very cheap price, to ensure a quick sale. He would take deposits from at least six or seven people and sometimes, if he could get away with it, even the full amount. He used to tell them that his brother was delivering a new wagon to him the fol-lowing day or so and that he would need to hand over the cash, promising them that he would move all his goods into the new wagon and then bring the wagon they would be buying to where they lived. He would give them a receipt, signed with a false name, of course. That's how he did his bit.

The daughter, Diana, was in her early twenties and

a stunning-looking girl with beautiful big green eyes. She knew how to dress and make the most of herself. Her speciality was to become engaged, and she could sometimes hook a man in just one or two days. The object here, of course, was the ring. Diana would first find her mark, which was easy for her, especially in small villages, as the males did not often see a woman swanning around looking like a film star, all high heels, beautifully done nails and well-coiffured hair. Some said that she'd been at this lark since she was about fifteen. One thing she did *not* do, from what we heard, was sleep with her victims.

Once she'd hooked her victim with her stunning looks, it was child's play to get him to ask her out. She would complain about her strict father and how unhappy she was. It wasn't long before the victims would be under her spell and feeling very protective. She would shyly confess to them that she had fallen immediately in love. As soon as she had the chap conditioned, she would lead him to the nearest jeweller's to pick out a ring, varying the price depending on the wealth of the man involved.

No, she didn't run off with the ring. She was cleverer than that.

Once she had the ring on her finger, she would go for a long walk with her victim, leading him either to a stream or somewhere where there was tall grass.

Then she would pick an argument and, in a temper, she would pull off her ring, throw it and storm off. She'd leave the bewildered victim searching for the ring, having seen it, with his own eyes, flying through the air. Except that this wasn't the real ring, but a cheap paste one bought from Woolworths. Even if he found that ring, he would keep searching, as he would know it was not the one that he had bought and placed on her finger.

The trickster family would then sneak out of the village in the middle of the night. As far as I know, they never were caught.

When spring came, the family headed back to Skegness. On the bracing east coast, away from the frightened towns, there was a different atmosphere, Depression or no. The gorgers were on holiday to forget their troubles, be it for a day or a week.

The girls had discovered an open-air theatre along the beach called the Arcadia where, every day, talent competitions were held. The sisters, though used enough to making their own entertainment and joining in with fellow Romanies, had never really experienced this kind of theatre before, where they could perform before the public. And this was exactly what they decided to do, having watched the gorgers' attempts at singing and dancing, which, to be honest, they found rather amateur.

They had been brought up singing and dancing every night and so were miles ahead when it came to experience and training. Mummy and Vera would tap dance together and had worked out many routines to their favourite songs. Lena, with her Marlene Dietrich-style voice, would sing 'Underneath the Lamplight'.

They knew, of course, that their parents would never have consented, so it took quite a bit of daring each other before one of them eventually went on stage. Sure enough, Lena won the Talent of the Day prize. Thereafter, it became a little monotonous as, day after day, one talented sister appeared after another, and it must have seemed to an increasingly restive audience (for they weren't all day-trippers) that this was some kind of benefit for the Petulengro family.

The manager was in fact accused of this, after all five of the older girls had won the contest in turn and were happily queuing up ready to win again. He called them aside and tactfully suggested that they were more or less monopolising his theatre, not to mention scaring off the talent among the holidaymakers, which it was the purpose of the show to encourage. The girls were a little sad, but they understood and, in any case, there were new horizons ahead. A number of professional talent spotters, or people who claimed they were, had already approached them after their appearances, offering them jobs in show business.

This would never be more than a dream, they knew, but the idea was thrilling and they were proud and flattered that they had been asked. The manager of the Arcadia was impressed too and he couldn't see why they shouldn't have their chance. Thinking to give them a pleasant surprise and not knowing anything about Romanies, he found out where Naughty's caravan was parked and went to see him. He congratulated him on his beautiful and talented daughters and told him that he would like to be their manager and give them training for careers on the stage.

Although he listened politely, Naughty's face froze as the mystery caller talked. At first he thought the manager must be a gorger lunatic, rambling on sense-lessly. Then, as the penny dropped that it really was his precious daughters the man was talking about and that they had been performing on stage in front of a lot of gorgers, he began to feel his blood boil. He somehow managed to calm himself down and remain polite, although his negative answer was so emphatic the manager realised he was not to be argued with.

When the girls came home, they took one look at their father's face and realised they'd been rumbled. They were lucky they shared the blame equally and Naughty didn't know which one to start with. For some reason, though, he did not get as angry as he thought he would; he felt more sadness in his heart, for he realised that this was another turning point. On the road, always travelling, this would never have happened. In the intimate confines of the vardos there were no secrets to be kept from each other, no chances to conspire. Things were different now.

It is true that the Romanies know little of culture outside of music and dancing; literature and art are not part of our lives, but we are all artistic in our own way. One particularly important craft among Romanies was always that of woodcarving, a practice put to good use making toys, bender tents and pegs for hawking. Our arts, or skills, are on the whole practical; we do not take a commercial view of them, as this story shows.

One day the family was pulled up near to a farm and the farmer, knowing the Romany reputation, asked Naughty to attend to one of his sick horses. Naughty worked through the night on the horse and managed to save its life, much to the relief of the farmer, whose favourite mare it was.

Naughty refused payment, for they were parked up on the farmer's land and it was what he would have done for any sick animal. But the farmer was adamant that he should have something for his night's work and, taking Naughty into the living room of the farmhouse, he insisted that he choose one of two paintings that hung there as a reward.

It was not a difficult choice for Naughty since one

of the paintings was a seascape and the other was of a horse. The horse, naturally, was the one he chose and the farmer wrapped it up for him to take away, at the same time mentioning, quite casually, that it had no value at all but that the seascape was valued at a hundred guineas. But Naughty couldn't have cared less. He couldn't understand why someone would want to hang an ugly picture on the wall just because it was worth lots of money!

In spite of the social restrictions placed on the girls, particularly by Naughty, there were no bars to their enjoyment of life, and as time went on, one by one they fell in love and married. Cissie, the eldest, was the first. The family moved to a winter stopping ground alongside the Lees and a mutual attraction sprang up between her and a young man called Laurence, so they eloped. If this sounds disrespectful to her parents, that wasn't the case at all. Eloping is the traditional Romany way.

The courtship of the Romany is vastly different from that of the gorger. Even now, a Romany girl is a virgin when she marries. She marries one man for life, and even if widowed when young, it is unlikely that she will marry again. This is not preached as a virtue, it is simply understood as one. We are brought up in a society which has strict moral standards and we think and behave in that way, as did our parents and grandparents and theirs before them. The close, tight-knit Romany society has not been exposed to, nor is it receptive to, the changes that have characterised the gorger way of life. If, in some ways, we are now reluctantly being drawn into the gorger society, these walls of strict morality, which we built to protect the purity of our Romany life, will be the last to crumble.

Marriages are not arranged, but usually the parents will have a mate in mind for their sons or daughters. When they think the time is right they will make sure that they and their prospective in-laws are travelling in the same direction, thus allowing a discreet meeting between boy and girl, safely supervised by two sets of parents.

When my mother was travelling, young people were allowed to look at each other, so long as the looks were not too familiar, and the first stage of casting glances went on for quite a while. They would eventually move on to talking, but would certainly never go out with each other. Even to be seen alone together would straight away set the elders asking questions, and any answers had to be good ones.

There is nothing immoral about the elopement and there is no sex involved; it is simply a commitment on the part of the young couple. They are not considered married, nor do they consider themselves married, until the Romany ceremony has taken place, regardless of whether they have been through a ceremony in a church or a register office or anywhere else. Every member of my family has eloped, including me. It is the way in which a Romany man claims his bride. Traditionally, they run off to the nearest group of Romanies, where they spend the night. Separately, of course.

Aunt Lena was the next to get married, to Terence Hewitt. Terence and his family were from Great Yarmouth and they had known each other for a long time through their families. The Hewitts were a good Romany family, as were the Herons of Blackpool. Vera married Cardy Heron when they were both nineteen. Then Adeline fell in love with Sydney Holt, who was a gorger, which initially caused quite a bit of commotion in the family. But he soon took to the Romany way of life and proved himself to be a wonderful husband to Adeline, so it wasn't long before he was well and truly accepted into the fold. It was now only my mother and Shunty who were yet to find husbands.

SEVEN

Secret Liaisons

Skegness was bustling in the summer of 1936. At Ingoldmells, Billy Butlin had opened his first ever holiday camp, in what was once a farmer's field, housing his guests in rows of chalets and providing food and entertainment for the sum of thirty-five shillings a week. The family must have been busier than ever that season, with the influx of holiday camp guests to the Butlins amusement park, but they were coping with sadness too.

That year Naughty had suffered two strokes. It was hard for them to see this once vigorous man, with his twinkling eyes, laid low. Granny always said that she blamed the fact they had stopped travelling for his illness. When they travelled, he walked for miles most days, had good food and lots of fresh air. Once they settled down, he seemed to start shutting down too.

On 27 June, Aunty Vera gave birth to her first child, a little girl. When he was told the news, Naughty asked that she be named Honour, after his mother. He died three days later from a third stroke. He was only sixty years old.

He was buried at Gorleston cemetery, alongside other members of his family, and Granny chose a big white marble angel as his headstone.

His death was not something Granny talked about – she preferred to remember the many happy years they'd shared. But I can imagine how devastated she must have been and also how she must have forced herself to stay strong for the sake of her family.

More change was on the way the following summer, when my mother met my father, Eddie Price. He was born in Nottingham in 1913. His father was a tailor and his mother died when he was young. Now aged twenty-three, Eddie was his own man, without a care in the world. He was working at the Butlins amusement park, erecting the hall of mirrors, when, strolling through the crowds one day, he saw a pretty girl standing by the entrance to Madam Eva's palmistry booth, getting some sun while waiting for customers.

He took her by surprise when he tried to talk to her, and she immediately noticed something about him that she'd never noticed in anyone else before. Something intriguing, even captivating. She felt herself blush and an urge came over her to talk to this young man to find out who he was. But, knowing she'd be in trouble if her brothers caught her, Mummy told him to go away. Every day for three days he walked that way again, hoping to see her, but each day one of the other sisters was working there instead.

One evening he took himself off to the dance hall at the holiday camp and there, by happy coincidence, he found my mother again. She was with several of the travelling girls from the amusement park and her eagle-eyed brothers, but there was no objection to her dancing. They spotted each other immediately and exchanged glances, so when the band struck up 'I've Got You Under My Skin', my father seized his chance. He asked her for a dance and she agreed. Mummy tried to avert her gaze while she danced with him, but every now and then, when she thought he wasn't looking, she'd peek up at this stranger who had made such an impression on her. Eddie was an attractive man, resembling some of the South American heartthrobs she had seen in the movies. With his slicked-back hair and his pencil moustache, he was obviously a bit of a lad, or so Uncle Nathan thought disapprovingly. Still, Mummy was having fun for what felt like the first time in her life and she was determined to enjoy every minute of it.

My father did his best to monopolise her for the rest of the evening. He knew better than to go outside the grounds of what was right, but over the next few weeks he did manage to make himself Mummy's regular dancing partner. He tried to make friends with her brothers too, but they knew that he was carrying a torch for their sister and they went out of their way to discourage him as much as possible. He was far too cocky for their liking and wasn't even Romany, so anything more than a dance was out of the question.

Aware of this hostility, the couple managed to snatch a number of short, secret meetings on the promenade during the summer. Before too long, Daddy proposed to Mummy and, almost to her surprise, she accepted. She was too terrified to tell her family anything about it. But they went ahead and, as the season was drawing to an end, made the necessary arrangements, and one morning they took the plunge and were quickly and secretly married in a gorger church.

Still, Mummy was too frightened to tell anyone and, despite Daddy's pleadings, she actually continued to live at home as a single girl for six whole weeks until, one day, she managed to pluck up enough courage to tell her mother. Granny insisted that the young man be brought before her immediately.

My mother went to get my father and she led him into the field where the family wagons were resting. There was a whole crowd of Romanies jostling around him and he thought for a moment that he was actually going to get lynched.

Granny's first words to the newlyweds before her

were 'You horrible little people.' But she followed this up with a stern question to Daddy: 'What will you have to drink?'

'I'll have a whisky please,' he said, in as confident a voice as he could muster.

'You'll have a beer like the rest of my sons!' Granny snorted.

My father knew then that, even though there was still a stern inquisition ahead, he had been accepted into the family. He followed meekly when Granny beckoned him inside the vardo, where he was interrogated about himself, his people, what he'd done and what he was intending to do. The cross-examination ended with a grim warning that if he ill-treated his wife, he would be a dead man. And on that cheerful note, they became friends.

Then came the Romany wedding ceremony. In this, the couple mingled blood by pricking their thumbs with a pin or a needle, as Indians do when they become blood brothers. Daddy was made to jump over fire and water, which seemed like child's play compared to the interrogation he had just been subjected to. This was to signify that he would go through any dangers for his new bride. All of this was accompanied by heavy drinking and a great deal of hilarity, though Romanies take the meaning of the ceremony with great seriousness.

Since my parents had not eloped, they had to do so now. While the party and the toasts were proceeding merrily, they slipped away to Daddy's small flat on the other side of town. At last they could start married life, even though they had now been legally married for over six weeks!

They can't have ever really talked about what they thought their married life would be like. I know Mummy assumed that they would live as Romanies, and they only lived in my father's flat for a couple of weeks before they borrowed Granny's old wooden vardo which would be their home for a number of years. I suspect it was all an adventure to begin with for my father, who was very impulsive. Perhaps he didn't understand what he was taking on – a large family with close ties, a way of life that existed alongside but separate from his own society, with strict rules of behaviour. When I was older, I always sensed he felt out of place with Romany men, who tended to talk obsessively about their horses and the next horse fair, neither of which held any interest for my father.

I was born on 18 March 1939, in Granny's painted caravan, in the same bed my mother had been born in. That month Hitler invaded what was left of Czechoslovakia, and Britain and France promised to support Poland should Germany turn its greedy eyes in that direction. On 1 September 1939 Germany did indeed invade Poland. Britain and France demanded they withdraw and when their ultimatum was rejected, on 3 September, we declared war.

It was inevitable that men of fighting age would soon be conscripted into the army. Many Romany men didn't feel part of British society. They asked for nothing and took nothing, but, as they saw it, they exchanged their talents for money and paid their own way. They didn't want to join the army and fight for a cause they did not see as their own. As they travelled around so much, my uncles had become somewhat untraceable – and didn't have birth certificates anyway – so they weren't conscripted as some Romanies were.

But, of course, my father was not a Romany. It may be that he was patriotic, or it may be that, at the age of twenty-six, he saw war as another adventure, a chance to escape his life. I will never know. But before he could be conscripted, my father went ahead and enlisted. My mother couldn't understand why he was so eager to volunteer for the army, and to leave behind both her and his baby girl.

EIGHT

Cowboys in Dunkirk

Daddy wanted to take my mother and me to Nottingham, to be near his family while he was away. She refused because she wanted to be near her own family in Spalding and in the end Daddy reluctantly agreed. But he insisted that Mummy's vardo should stay in Weldon's car park, rather than behind the Red Lion with Granny and the others. My mother couldn't understand why he wanted this, but it seemed a small price to pay.

After Daddy had left, a travelling man that my parents knew well came to see Mummy at their vardo in Spalding, to see if she could stop him being sick.

'You have to help me,' he said. 'It's my stomach – the cramps, the pain. It's terrible. I just can't bear it anymore.'

'I can help you,' she said, 'if you tell me what you've taken.'

'Nothing,' he moaned, his hands gripping his shirt tightly.

'OK,' said Mummy, 'then I'm afraid you'll have to go and see a doctor in the town, as there is nothing I can do for you if you won't tell me the truth.' She turned on her heels and headed back up the steps to the vardo.

'Wait,' shouted the man. 'Help me.'

'Like I said,' Mummy replied, 'I can't help you if you don't tell me what you've taken.'

She was no fool and had seen enough illnesses in her time to know that this one was self-inflicted. She also knew that if he hadn't taken something, he would have gone to the local hospital and not come to her vardo begging for mercy. She shut the top door to the vardo with a bang.

'All right,' the man groaned. 'I did take something.'

With a creak, the vardo door opened again. 'Sit down,' Mummy said, gently but firmly. She went into the wagon and returned with her Uncle Walter's trin mixture. 'Trin' is the Romany word for three, and the mixture was made up of three ingredients. What those ingredients were, I was never told.

'I just couldn't go to war, you see. I couldn't face leaving my wife. She's sick and can't take care of our daughter on her own. Now I can't even take care of myself, let alone my family.' Mummy had been hearing tales like this since conscription began.

'What did they tell you it would do to you if you took it?' she asked calmly.

'They said it would make my heart race, so that I wouldn't pass the medical. It did, it worked, but I was so nervous, I took more than they told me to, and now . . . and now . . .' The man bent over and let out a shriek of pain. If he hadn't been of the male gender, it would have appeared that he was having labour pains.

'You're lucky,' smiled Mummy, brandishing the bottle of trin mixture. 'We have just about enough left to sort you out, young man.'

A few days later, she had a visitor. It was a very smartly dressed young man who, had he not looked so chipper and happy, would have reminded her of the bent-up man on her steps a few days before. One more glance and she could see that it was, in fact, the very same man.

'Good morning,' he said, with a large grin on his face.

'Well, good morning to you too,' said Mummy. 'You sure do look a lot better than you did a few days ago.'

'I feel it too,' he said, with relief in his voice. 'Now I've come to see if I can put a smile on your face too.' With this, he whisked a large bag from behind his back. From it he produced a silver tea service that had belonged to his mother and two whole fillets of steak. The whole family dined well that night!

My father, meanwhile, had been made a despatch rider, which suited him fine. He liked playing about with engines and knew he could always cope with any mechanical emergencies. Astride his motorbike, he was on his own and free, which is how he liked to be. He was sent to France in 1939, where the British Expeditionary Force were hunkered down ready to repel any German invasion. Riding from one camp to another delivering messages was a simple and straight-forward task – for a while anyway. Nothing much happened for months until, on 10 May 1940, German troops swept through Belgium and headed for France. British and French forces were unable to hold them back, and by 26 May the British Expeditionary Force were almost surrounded. They managed to hold open a corridor to the sea at Dunkirk and that's where the army headed, hoping for evacuation.

Later, when he came back to England, my father told Mummy of his experiences, and particularly the horrors of Dunkirk. When they got the order to retreat, he was rather better off than the others, for at least he had his bike, he told her. But he was not so lucky on one particular day. A swooping dive-bomber caused him to skid off the road and, although he was unhurt, his bike was a total write-off. So he started to walk past the mound of bodies – the men, very often young boys, who had not managed to find shelter in the ditches when the German planes bombed or machine-gunned them.

He tried to thumb a lift, but without success. All the trucks on the road were more than packed, often with wounded soldiers, so he resigned himself to the prospect of a long walk. It was horrifying, trudging along that corpse-lined road, weary to the point of dropping, until the sound of approaching enemy aircraft produced vigour from nowhere, unknown strength to power a dive for safety.

It came as a surprise when a slow, grinding truck did stop, without even being thumbed. The truck was loaded with equipment and the driver was a soldier named Jack Whittaker. Anybody who had offered my father a lift when he was at the point of near exhaustion would have seemed like a bosom friend, but he and Jack really did hit it off. Jack had always been intrigued by Romany life and was fascinated to find someone who knew all about it.

They got so involved in their conversation that Jack missed seeing a crater at the edge of the road. The truck's front wheels dipped into it and, before Jack could wrestle with the wheel and straighten out, they tipped off the road and collided with a tree. The tree survived; the truck did not. It was yet another write-off and this time not even the Germans could be blamed.

So it was back to the foot-slogging again, but for my father, it was not such a long walk as before. Less than a kilometre up the road, he spotted, in a distant field, some French artillery horses which had been set loose. They were without saddles or harnesses, but that didn't worry Daddy. Jack, who had often in civilian life pined for the romantic gypsy existence, found himself being instructed in bareback riding, though in rather less glamorous circumstances than he had ever dreamed about.

So off they went and they must have been a sight, the two of them, jogging along the road to Dunkirk like a couple of cowboys. They weren't unaware of the humour of the situation, but there was a lot that was very unfunny as well. It was getting dark now, but they dared not stop. They had to press on, even if it meant travelling all night. It was pretty clear that the Germans were not far away, and neither had the slightest fancy to be shot or finish up in a prisoner of war camp.

My father was obviously much the better horseman, but, he said, it was not Jack's fault when his horse slithered and lost its footing, then rolled into a ditch with Jack still on its back.

Jack was all right, but the horse was screaming and my father knew immediately that the poor creature had broken a leg. His own mount was panicking now and becoming quite hysterical, so they both knew there was only one thing to do. He shot the two horses and would always be haunted by the expression in those poor animals' eyes, even more than by the memory of the blind eyes of the dead men who lined that road to Dunkirk.

Back on foot, the two of them stumbled on through the dark until their next misfortune, when my father tripped over something on the verge of the road and fell head-first into a water-logged ditch. Jack jumped in to help him and they clambered out, but both of them were soaked through to the skin. It was incredibly cold, which left only one course open to them and, although they felt like scavengers, they had to take it. They searched around, found some corpses of about the right build and took clothes from them. A French officer provided my father with a pair of trousers, but there was a huge hole in the back of the tunic. Nearby, however, he found an overcoat on a British major who was sadly long past feeling the cold of the night.

Dry at last in their new clothes, but weary almost to the point of exhaustion, they trudged on till they got to a NAAFI base. There was plenty of food and drink there, but all they wanted to do was sleep and they practically collapsed on the spot.

At daylight, when they woke, they were eager to

My beloved granny, Alice Eva Petulengro. She was a tiny woman, who was also incredibly strong, brave and open-minded. Smart as a carrot and always beautifully groomed, she carried herself with the poise of a duchess.

My grandfather, Naughty Petulengro, so-called because of the mischievous twinkle in his eye. He is pictured here, on the left, with his brother Olby in Skegness.

The men in my family all loved their Aptus cameras! From left to right are Frank Taylor, Uncle Alger and Uncle Nathan.

Aunt Adeline, sitting on the steps of Granny's vardo (caravan). Her beautiful green-brown eyes were said to change colour every time you looked at her.

Aunt Vera standing next to my mother, Laura Eva, outside a bender tent, which would be used to give them more space when the vardos were parked up.

Aunt Cissie, sitting on the left, was known as the most beautiful of my mother's sisters. Behind her is Uncle Alger, while Uncle Nathan and Aunt Lena can be seen on the right.

My beautiful mother, Laura Eva, at the age of nineteen. She was never one to show her emotions openly, but that didn't stop an incredible bond from developing between us. She meant the world to me.

And here she is with my aunt Vera. The two girls were inseparable as they were growing up.

Granny's vardo. My grandfather, Naughty, carefully selected each piece of wood that went into the building of it, and oversaw the wood carving and mirror engravings inside, determined to have only the best for Granny.

Skegness, 1940. My father, Eddie, was home on leave from the war, visiting me, aged one, and my mother.

Shortly after my mother and
father were married, Granny gave them
her vardo, which became our home for
many years to come. Here I am, aged
two, sitting on the steps, while Mummy
checks on me from the window.

Aunt Shunty, the youngest of
my mother's sisters, who would often
look after me when I was little. I used to
look at Shunty and wish that one day
I might be as beautiful as her.

Mummy pushing her beloved Silver Cross pram. I'm standing by her side, aged nine, as we take the twins, Eddie and Anne, for a walk.

Me, aged twelve, with Eddie. I would often entertain the twins while Mummy gave readings to clients.

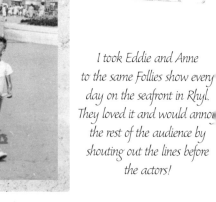

I took Eddie and Anne to the same Follies show every day on the seafront in Rhyl. They loved it and would annoy the rest of the audience by shouting out the lines before the actors!

continue on their journey, but they took advantage of their situation by loading up with as many cigarettes as they could reasonably carry. When they got back onto the main Dunkirk road, there was the usual sight of battle-weary troops beating their bedraggled way towards the coast and, out of pity for them, my father and Jack stood at the side of the road and handed out cigarettes from their plentiful store. To my father's surprise, all the men saluted him, although he was not looking for more than a word of thanks. It took him quite a while before he realised, to his and Jack's amusement, that it was, of course, the major's overcoat they were saluting.

At least they felt they were giving their fellow Tommies a bit of heart, as they travelled on their dismal route. But later that same day they witnessed an incident which really gave a new lease of life to those footsore and dispirited soldiers. The Scots Guards had been through just as much as all the other troops, but they decided that they were going to set an example of how to retreat with dignity. When they marched to Dunkirk, their uniforms were smart, the soldiers clean and shaved. They marched like guardsmen and ahead of them was their band, in full dress uniform, playing their bagpipes. It must have seemed like a mirage to some of those men but, as an example, it certainly worked. Bearded and grubby soldiers, even the most cynical among them, raised a cheer for the Scotsmen and then, with new heart, joined in the march towards Dunkirk. Retreating or not, they were doing it with pride.

When they got to the beach of embarkation, their problems were not over by any means. Indeed, it seemed as though they were just beginning. The dive-bombers were coming in regularly and the thousands of British soldiers, herded onto the beach like cattle, were easy pickings for them. Although just about everything that could sail, from tiny dinghies to cross-Channel steamers, had put out from England, as well as the navy's own ships, there was still the enormous task of getting everyone on board while under heavy fire, and particularly of getting the wounded away first.

Daddy and Jack decided to move into the town, for a bit anyway, since the bombings seemed to be concentrated on the beach. While there, he met some French gypsies with whom he was able to converse in the Romany language common to them. The Frenchmen knew that it was like a slaughterhouse on the beach and they offered to garrave (hide) them. But my father's only desire was to see the back of France now, for he had just about had enough. All he wanted was to see his home and his family again, and he was quite prepared to risk his life for that.

So it was back to the beaches, and there he had

another strange meeting, this time with a man called Gadsby, whom he knew from Skegness. Gadsby was a performer – he used to high-dive from the pier into a ring of flame on the water. My father couldn't have asked for a more appropriately qualified friend than this and he made sure he stuck close by him. They finally managed to get on a boat together and, as it happened, they weren't more than a few hundred yards out to sea when it hit a mine and sank. Gadsby saved several men who couldn't swim while my father was dog-paddling his way back to the beach. He, Gadsby and most of the survivors managed to get aboard a second boat and, again, they had hardly got clear of the beach when they suffered a direct hit from a German dive-bomber, the bomb going clean down the steamer's funnel. Yet another scramble took place and once more Gadsby played a heroic part, saving more lives because of his skill as a diver and swimmer.

By now, as can be imagined, it was like Bedlam at the beach, with hundreds of small ships arriving, more and more troops converging on Dunkirk from the battle lines and the Germans throwing in every dive-bomber and fighter they had, pausing their ferocious onslaught only to refuel and rearm. Dozens of ships were being sunk and the survivors machine-gunned in the water as they tried to get back to the beach.

In the midst of the chaos, Daddy got separated from

his friends, but managed to get a place on board – of all the ridiculous vessels that were there in Dunkirk harbour – a paddle boat normally used for pleasure trips between coastal resorts like Margate and Ramsgate. The *King George V* was not built for speed or for manoeuvrability, but it somehow managed to evade the minefields and the German dive-bombers, and paddled, literally, its way back home.

One day in the NAAFI canteen, while queuing up for a meal, my father heard a welcome and familiar sound. One of the men on fatigues was mumbling away to himself, cursing miserably, as he splashed out dollops of mashed potatoes. There was nothing unusual in that except that the man was cursing in Romany, which made my father smile.

'Keker puker duver, chore,' he said. ('Don't speak like that, boy.') The man cheered up immediately, hardly able to believe his own ears, and could not wait until he was able to join my father for a chat. The Romany boy's name was Leo Cooper and he was one of those who had been called up, much against his will. He felt a tremendous resentment against the army and was terribly homesick, finding it impossible to make friends among the gorgers. He poured out all his troubles to my father.

His young wife was expecting her first child and was unable to earn her keep. Most Romany women work for the full term of their pregnancy, but Leo's wife was having a bad time and he desperately wanted to get home to her. 'I've got to jaw kerry,' he kept repeating. ('I've got to go home.') Daddy warned him of the dangers of desertion, but Leo was determined. He felt he just had to get back and take his wife somewhere where at least she would not be lonely and would have her relatives to care for her. But he had no intention of coming back, even then, because he hated the disciplines of army life. He wanted to be free again.

In fact, Leo was better off than he thought and the job he had in the cookhouse was one which was much sought after. It was always warm, there was plenty to eat, and the cooks were excused from all drills and guard duties.

The day after Leo's chat with my father, they were a man short in the cookhouse. At the same time, by a strange coincidence, Daddy was enquiring whether there was a vacancy for a cook. He always had a silver tongue and, when asked what his qualifications were, he told such a beautiful and mouth-watering tale that he not only got a job, they put him in charge!

Since he had never so much as boiled an egg in his whole life, this was something of a problem, and one that he hadn't bargained for. He had not known, when he applied, that the NCO in charge of the place was being posted to some other camp. Ever quick-witted, though, he realised that he could turn the situation to his advantage. Being in charge meant he didn't actually have to do any cooking, which is when he would have been in danger of being found out. All he had to do now was to convince the cooks that he knew what he was doing and he would be all right.

So he marched up and down the cookhouse as though he were the head chef at the Savoy or somewhere, barking at the youngest and most inexperienced of the men to start with.

'What d'you think you're doing, lad?' was his favourite question. The young cook would then nervously launch into a long and detailed description, which was exactly what my father wanted, as it enabled him to learn. All his close attention to the work was perceived as conscientious inspection by the chefs and he rapidly gained the respect of the men for what they believed to be his astute supervision.

He realised, of course, that this might not wash with the older and more experienced men working there. He gave them a wide berth for a day or two until he managed to get out into the surrounding fields and gather together a collection of vegetables and herbs used by Romany women in their cooking: onions, wild thyme, fennel, marjoram and garlic. Then, copying his wife, he sprinkled a handful of herbs into this dish and that one, improving the flavour considerably. Since army cooking was very basic, any improvement was a huge success. The men enjoyed their food and the cynical cooks developed a great respect for Daddy, who they thought had to be some kind of expert.

Learning fast, Daddy rapidly did become an expert – so far as army cooking was concerned anyway. As well as herbs and vegetables, he would gather mushrooms, which normally never figured on any army menu, and these he reserved for the sergeants' mess, where he became very popular indeed.

From this point onwards, his life in the army was pretty comfortable.

NINE

Who's This Man I Call Daddy?

Keeping me out of mischief was obviously a major concern of the adults around me. Granny would often have first shift of the day, taking me with her to the bakery across the road from the Red Lion. She would make her own bread and take it over to the baker, who'd put it in his oven. An hour or so later, she'd go back to collect it. I loved the smell in the shop – freshly baked bread mixed with the sugary aroma of the cakes laid out on the counter. Granny would leave with a big basket of still-warm loaves and I'd be clutching a fresh cake in my hand – the best way to keep me quiet.

I'd also be given odd jobs to do. I was probably more of a nuisance than I was worth, but the grown-ups cleverly managed to give me the impression that I was doing something really useful. In Romany families, children are set to work at an early age, not in order to exploit them, but to give them a feeling of belonging in their society and as an introduction to the skills they'll need later for survival. Their contribution is quite useful, however. The men would be away working during the day and the women would go out hawking, going from door to door selling clothes pegs and offering readings. In older days, the little boys would tend the horses, while girls were sewing, cleaning and preparing meals long before the age of ten.

The whole family is part of the Romany community and each family is a small community of its own. The children know when times are hard and money is scarce. They also know when things are going well and share in the good times with their parents. In gorger houses, there are many different rooms with doors behind which family members often hide from each other. A secret is like a veil which hides part of your personality. Wear enough veils and you will become unrecognisable. In this way, the members of a family can become strangers to one another.

There can be few secrets in a vardo. As a child, you hear all of the discussions about where and how your family will earn the next lot of money and, in this way, you eventually learn to plan your own enterprises. You find out what things cost early on and what they can be sold for. Bargaining among the traders, you learn quite a bit. If you heard a gorger boy of about twelve, say, talk to a Romany boy the same age, you would probably describe the Romany boy as being like a little adult, because he would be so sharp in some matters, especially anything to do with money. Even when things are going well, the pressure is always on you to work harder, do better and put more money away for the future.

Sitting around outside the wagon, I'd watch as my uncle Nathan carved so expertly the clothes pegs which my mother and her sisters would later take out to their clients. The other men in the family would join in, sitting on the steps of the vardo, bantering about who was the best and the quickest at carving, laughing and racing each other. Below the steps, a large canvas sheet would catch the wood shavings and I'd watch mesmerised as they started to mount up. They used willow, which was shaved and then cut into lengths of four or five inches, which were then split in half to make the peg. A pile of Colman's mustard tins were stacked against the side of the vardo and these were cut into tiny strips and tacked onto the wood to make the joint of the peg. Then the pegs were shaped and finished and it was my job to put them together into little bundles.

The women in the family actually made a really good living selling pegs. A hawking licence was not necessary if the goods being sold were homemade, so there was no conflict with the law or any local authority. And often visits to the various houses led to hand-reading sessions, which were more lucrative than selling clothes pegs and a lot more interesting.

I was often left in the care of Shunty, my mother's youngest sister, who also cleaned up the vardo and helped to prepare our meals. I'd look at her, with her long, dark, curly hair worn over one eye like Veronica Lake, and hope that one day I'd be as beautiful. She had such an amazing manner about her and talked to me as if she was on the same level as me. It was her magical gift for making people feel at ease that would take her on to become one of the most popular palm-readers in Skegness. So much so that she went on to work well into her seventies.

Shunty always worked hard and was very kind-hearted, but she had a tongue as sharp as a knife if she was crossed by anyone. She stood no nonsense from her older brothers, but her arch-enemy was her cousin Frank Taylor, who lived nearby. A couple of years older than her, Frank was a snappy dresser, a handsome chap who always wore a big cheeky grin on his face. This didn't impress Shunty though. For some reason, it seemed as though they just hated each other on sight.

She claimed that he was always trying to annoy her and sparks would fly whenever they clashed in an argument, which was more often than not. Frank had his own vardo, which was parked next to that of his brother Willy and sister-in-law Bubbles. He had a great

99

affection for my grandmother and she, with the same affection, treated him like one of her own sons. In her wisdom, she obviously saw a lot more than any of us did and I think she knew that before many years had passed the arch-enemies would be happily wed!

Although the war was on and the Butlins holiday camp had been taken over by the navy, I do remember us still going to Skegness as the amusement park stayed open. In 1943 the elders sat down and held a meeting to discuss the coming season and Granny said, 'We can't leave some of you here; we all have to stick together. So if we go to Skegness, you've all got to come.' They readily agreed.

When entering Skegness at Easter, we would drive past the tulip fields – this area is called Little Holland. It was just like a patchwork quilt – a field of yellow, then a field of red, then blue, then purple and white. All the colours of the rainbow, each side of the narrow roads, stretching out forever. At each side of the road were drainage ditches and more than once we had seen cars that had been going too fast end up in one of them.

As we rode into Skegness, with the familiar sights of the beach and the sea, we felt as if we were coming home. The smell of the salt in the air made us feel alive again, awoke our senses and raised the spirits of the family, as they realised they could get back into their routine again. We weren't allowed on some of the beaches, though, due to the barbed wire and land mines.

Mummy told me years later that because Shunty, who was not yet fifteen, looked older than her age and was very good at the arts of palmistry and clairvoyance, Granny had decided that she could start work that summer. However, Shunty got into trouble because she went out and bought a whoopee cushion, the child in her always present. It may have been a serious job she was undertaking, but she was determined to have fun while doing it. She placed it on the client's chair and mischievously waited for the loud fart when they sat on it. Luckily, she couldn't get it to work – she must have been sold a duff one – but Granny found it when she came to relieve Shunty and was more than a little angry. 'We don't do pranks in such a serious business, child.' Shunty was barred from giving readings for a whole month after that. She didn't care, though; she was more upset that the cushion didn't work than the fact that she'd got into trouble for it.

Towards the end of the summer, my mother received a telegram to say that my father would be on leave from the army and would be in Skegness within two days. I was four and a half and I'd been promised that my daddy would take me round and buy me ice creams when he got back. As any child of my age would be,

I was very excited at this prospect and my best dress was laid out all ready for his arrival.

It's funny, isn't it, how you can love someone so much and then on some days you look and you just see a complete stranger? As I was growing up, I often saw these emotions register on my mother's face, just as they would begin to register on mine when I saw a loving father one minute and then someone I didn't recognise the next.

I remember very well, even though I was so young, that I was happy when he came home. The night he was due back seemed to drag on endlessly and no matter how hard I tried to keep my eyes open, it wasn't long before sleep got the better of me. I awoke to hear noises outside and see my new dress laid at the foot of my bed. My tummy turned over with excitement at the thought of the delights of the day to come. I could almost taste the ice cream and feel the warmth of his hand holding mine.

When I came out of the vardo, all of the family were seated around a stick fire having their breakfast, including my mother and father. I ran up to Daddy and put my arms around his neck. He turned and gave me a smile and I felt as if my world was complete again. After a while, my mother and her sister piled into a car and Uncle Nathan drove them down to the amusement park to work, with calls of 'See you later' and 'Have a good day.' At last I was alone with my father.

'Come on, get what you need, we're going out,' he said.

I rushed up into the vardo and grabbed my hairbrush. I hurriedly ran it through my hair and checked my appearance in the mirror. I picked up my cardigan and, smiling, stood on the steps of the vardo, looking down into my daddy's eyes.

'Jump, Eva,' he said, smiling. 'I'll catch you.'

I stepped forward trustingly, prepared to be caught up in my father's arms. Before I knew it, I hit the ground with a smack and felt the mud slowly but surely soaking into my clothes.

He had moved out of the way. I was devastated and, as the tears started to come from my eyes, I looked down at his shoes and then up his legs and into those very same eyes which had seconds ago promised me safety and love. Now they were narrowed and, with pursed lips, he said, 'Let that be a lesson to you. Never trust anyone.'

He turned on his heels and walked away. How could he do that to me? How could he trick his little girl?

Later, when I was back with Mummy, she wanted to know why I was covered in mud. When I told her, I saw a look in her eyes, fury followed by sadness, something I'd never seen before.

After the incident on the wagon steps, my father kept his distance for a few days, so when he asked me if I'd like him to teach me to swim, I jumped at the chance. Maybe he wasn't as mean as I'd just been led to believe. I was always desperate for his approval or attention, glad of any sign that I could be his girl and he could be the kind of father my cousins Daisy and Honour had in Uncle Cardy.

He brought me down to the beach and walked me across the golden sands to the edge of the water. Laughing out loud, he picked me up and swung me round. This was fun! He put me down, took off his shoes and rolled up his trouser legs. He picked me up again and waded into the sea with me. All of a sudden, without any warning, he threw me into the sea. Just before I hit the water, I heard him shout, 'Now swim!'

I remember the water going up my nose and down my throat and I can still feel the sense of panic I felt when I realised my feet didn't touch the seabed. My arms were flailing, but I was going nowhere but down. I felt as if I was dropping to the bowels of the sea.

Eventually, I was picked up by my father and dropped onto the sand, where I must have lain sobbing and snorting for at least twenty minutes. I could still feel the soreness of my throat from the salty water which I had swallowed in bucketfuls.

I couldn't see what my father was doing because I

was still crying so hard and the salt in my eyes had blurred my vision, but I know he didn't come to help me, nor did he comfort me.

Something changed in me that day. If this was my father, who was supposed to look after me and love me, then what were the rest of the people in the world like? I am sure that he is the reason I have distrusted so many people in the past, and still do. I can't believe that someone isn't going to let me down and hurt me just when I have learned to trust them. After all, he did. He was the first and last man to break my heart.

What makes someone like this? My mother always put my father's behaviour down to his time in Dunkirk. She was making a weak excuse, not for him, but for me, so that I wouldn't feel bad. It was many years later that I realised the real reason: the man simply did not know how to be a father. He did not have the instincts for it, nor did he wish to learn how.

That episode gave me nightmares for many years to come. I would dream of being back flailing in the sea and I would wake up with the sense that my nostrils and mouth were full of salt water.

When my mother found out what had happened to me, a major row followed and she told him she would not let me out with him on my own again. He simply smirked. Maybe this had been his plan all along? The next day – to my relief and, looking back, to my mother's – my father left to return to the army.

So my mother was left with my baby brother Nathan and myself. She would take us down to the palmistry place at Butlins with her every day and would pay some of the travelling girls to take us for walks while she read palms. And that was how life went on, at least for a while.

TEN

Hunting for Hotchis and a Handful of Herbs

I didn't know at the time how idyllic my childhood was, living the Romany life, surrounded by my family. I am sure there were hardships, but as a child you don't see them, do you? For instance, during the war food was rationed and obviously for my family ration books were tricky, because officially the Petulengros didn't exist. We weren't entitled to dole money or pensions either. Luckily, we were given temporary ration books and Mummy learned very quickly how to exchange readings for things that were on ration, stuff like clothing coupons and so on, which were effectively as good as money.

It was hard for everyone making do with the limited food available while things were being rationed. Once a week we were allowed meat up to the value of 1s 6d, 2oz of butter, cheese and tea, 8oz of sugar, 4oz of bacon and 1 egg per person. We were also allowed 12oz of sweets each month.

A lot of the fairground travellers used bleach to remove the stamps from their ration books so they could reuse them at the next village. Even gorgers began to do what they needed to do to survive this awful time in one piece. But I don't remember food ever being scarce; it was much easier for us Romanies as we were used to living off what nature has to offer to a certain extent. Granny kept chickens, so we always had fresh eggs, and my uncles would regularly go hunting. Uncle Nathan's speciality was catching hedge-hogs, and he could often be found poking about in the hedgerows with a stick, searching for the creature that we called the hotchi. They would usually be found curled up, like a bundle of dried grass, and when un-curled you would have to smack them on the nose with a stick. He had a knack of being able to do this quickly and accurately, making for a much less painful death for the creature. I couldn't bear to witness this going on and would always make myself scarce. The hotchi would have his prickles burned off by one of the boys, who would then cover it with wet clay and place it into the ashes of a stick fire. When the clay is baked, it's cracked open and the hotchi is pulled out of its mould of clay. The skin then comes away with it, leaving the baked hedgehog to eat. The flavour is a cross between pork and chicken. It may seem cruel, but when you think of all the other animals people eat, it is not that different. And food always tastes better eaten and cooked outside, over a stick fire.

Uncle Alger was the champion trout tickler, the fine art of rubbing the underbelly of the trout with skilful fingers. This would make the trout go into a trance-like state after a minute or two, enabling Alger to throw it onto the nearest bit of dry land. The beauty of this was that it required no nets, rods or lines. He would watch the fish working their way up the shallows and rapids and when his instinct told him to, he would take to the water, slow but sure, kneel on one knee and pass his hand, with his fingers up, under a rock, until he came into contact with the fish's tail. He would begin tickling with his forefinger, gradually running his hand along the fish's belly further and further towards the head, until his hand was under its gills. With a quick grasp and a struggle, he would wrench it out, stun it with a deft blow to the head and, if he had an audience, he would stick it in his pocket with a wry smile.

The men would also hunt fowl with catapults, which was an art taught to the boys from an early age, passed down from generation to generation.

Uncle Walter kept us healthy with his special gift for making herbal remedies – for animals and humans.

If someone was feeling under the weather, he would mix up some sarsaparilla chips, Spanish liquorice and Epsom salts for them, and order the patient to drink some every morning until it was gone. This would clean the blood and ensure that any sluggishness the person was feeling would disappear. His other famous recipes were for dandelion or feverfew tea, to cure headaches. Sometimes he would give people bark from the willow tree to hang around their necks. Some people would have called him a witch doctor, but these simple yet effective remedies still work today. Aspirin is made from willow bark, after all.

I'd wake up in the morning and hear Granny moving around, making breakfast. She'd take some bacon, or perhaps sausages, from the belly box that sat outside, underneath the back of the vardo, and was used to keep food cool. It was often called a hay box and was also used to transport the chickens and bantams when travelling.

As she cooked on the oven, she'd softly sing her favourite tune, 'Roses are Blooming in Picardy'. I'd sit on my bed, watching her nod in contentment, as she so often did when she was concentrating, or talking, or singing. The wonderful smell would drift to Mummy and Shunty in their vardo and they'd come to join us, bringing Nathan.

'Get that peamingre [tea] on, Shunty,' Granny would

shout. Sometimes one of my uncles' dogs, usually a whippet, would appear at the door, lured by the smell, and Granny would shoo it away. 'Jaw, you wafedi jukel.' ('Go away, bad dog.')

At night the family would sit down around the fire, our bellies full of rabbit stew simmered with freshly picked herbs. As the wood crackled, we children would eagerly wait to hear the tales our mothers and grandmothers loved to tell.

'Oh, Granny,' I'd say, 'please tell us the story of the nails again.' She must have told this tale a million times to her own children, but she'd sit down and begin the story her mother had told her, and hers had before her.

'When Jesus Christ was betrayed and handed over to the Romans and they were going to crucify him, no blacksmith in the city would forge the nails to do it with. The soldiers were sent to search further afield. They came across a band of Romanies who were parked up outside the city walls and the soldiers commissioned them to make four nails and said they would return the following day to collect them. The next day, when they arrived, the Romany smithy declared that he had only been able to make three nails. The angry soldiers said that they needed four and had to have them that day, as they were going to be crucifying Jesus. The

Romanies are very God-fearing people. They prayed at night and truly believed that Jesus was the son of God. At hearing what was to be done with the nails, the Romanies fled, and this is why Jesus was crucified with three nails instead of four.'

When Granny used to tell her own children this story, she'd put her hand to Naughty's neck and pull out a gold nail attached to a chain round his neck and it would shine in the light cast by the fire. As a horse-smith, he wore this good luck symbol, as do many Romany men.

Sometimes we'd be joined round the fire by more distant relatives and other Romany families and their friends. Celebrating births, weddings and even funerals was looked forward to, as it was a great chance to get together and gossip with faces you hadn't seen in months, if not years. There were also the horse fairs to attend, and gathering together at Christmas, when we could, was always a highlight. Each night the men would go to the alehouse to talk and drink, while the females would be left to their own devices, and would sit around the fire, laughing all night at remembered childhood antics and at bizarre stories they had recently heard. While gossiping, they'd give themselves beauty treatments and possibly drink the odd drop of gin from a teacup.

I remember sitting quietly round the fire listening

to Kyra, who was a distant cousin and who was always up to reminiscing about being beaten to within an inch of her life. In between giggling, she told the tale.

'It was me mother and father's wedding anniversary the next day, so I'd made an excuse that I wanted to go buy meself a blouse. So there I am, I've bought a nice present for their anniversary, a bit of cut glass, and as I come out the shop, this young man who pretended he knew me brother stopped me to ask how me brother was and how long we'd be staying in the village. I tried to get away from him, but he kept talking. I didn't know it, but me father's brother saw me stood talking to him. By the time I got home, me father was as mad as hell and asked me where I'd been. Well, I didn't want to tell him that I'd been to buy him a present, did I? His face was nearly black with anger and he went striding off up the field.

'Give me some more gin, dear,' Kyra held her cup out for a refill. 'Then I saw him coming towards me. He'd cut himself a stick and, even though I was eighteen years old, he whacked me something rotten on me legs and bum, because he thought I'd been making myself fair over a gorger boy.' All the girls started laughing at this, because they all knew the tale by now.

'I couldn't wait till the next morning,' Kyra started up again with a wry smile, 'to tell him why I'd been so long.' Kyra had, over the years, enhanced this story, because she loved to watch the faces of those who hadn't heard it before.

The next day, when he got his present, Kyra's father realised how he had misjudged her and was terribly upset. But that is Romany life. There is this strong protective instinct against strangers, the gorger above all.

One of Mummy's favourite stories concerned the telephone. When it comes to business, Romanies make frequent use of the phone, since this saves the time and embarrassment of trying to find someone who can write letters. She knew of one old Romany, though, Charlie, a very eccentric old boy, who just did not believe in the telephone. He was from a very well-thought-of family, but his wife had died, leaving behind her husband and their son Charlie Junior. The son dealt in motor cars and used to make telephone calls all over the place, finding new vehicles or looking for spare parts. Old Charlie found it very hard to cope with his wife's departure. They would travel with other families and, at night, old Charlie would take out his bike and go to the nearest public house. Once, when they were travelling, old Charlie asked young Charlie, 'What are these red boxes for?' pointing at a phone box.

Young Charlie explained, 'They're telephone boxes, Dad. You put some money in and you can phone people and talk to them, even if they're a long way away.'

Old Charlie took this with a pinch of salt. 'Charlie,

don't you try to tell me that with that thing you can talk to someone who's twenty miles away or more.' So young Charlie stopped trying to explain.

Anyway, on this particular night, after getting his fill of whisky at the pub, Old Charlie mounted his bicycle and started to pedal back to where they were camped. Unfortunately, due to his inebriated state, he ran into a red telephone box and buckled the front wheel. He sat on the grass, trying to work out whether he could walk the distance back to the camp, knowing he wouldn't be able to carry the bicycle and couldn't push it because the wheel was buckled. He sat pondering on this problem and then he looked at the box, went inside and examined the telephone. He took a tuppenny bit from his pocket, put it into the box and said down the receiver, 'Charlie, bring the car.'

This is where young Charlie found him when he came to look for him an hour later, worried that his father hadn't yet come home from the public house. Charlie Senior was sound asleep. Whether this tale is correct or not, it's been told many times by Charlie Junior.

Charlie Junior fell in love with a girl called Lisa. She loved him too, but her parents were dead against them even talking to one another, for Charlie's family was not pure Romany. This made life difficult for them, to say the least, but Charlie was very persistent. He used to find out what places Lisa's family was travelling to and then make a point of going there too, just to see her. The parents realised why he was always there, however, and did everything they could to keep them apart.

One evening, quite late, Lisa's family arrived at a stopping place and saw that Charlie's vardo and car were already there. They would have moved on there and then, but they were tired and the horses needed resting – they still had a horse-drawn vardo – and so they decided to stay but to set off very early the next morning.

Lisa managed to slip away from the vardo for a few minutes and found Charlie waiting for her. They were both frustrated at being kept apart and they decided there and then to elope, in the small hours of the morning, while her parents were sleeping. She managed to get away all right but, even before it was dawn, some instinct made Lisa's father get up and check to see if she was still there. He saw she was missing, guessed what was happening and woke his wife up at once. He knew they would be headed for the nearest town and he immediately hitched up the horses, ready to go after them.

The scene was set for a colourful drama, with the old Romany wagon hurrying through the half-light of approaching dawn, the horses spurred on by the grim-faced father seated up front, with his equally anxious wife next to him, worrying whether they would find their lost daughter in time to stop the wedding, which they were both convinced would be disastrous for her.

Lisa, travelling some miles ahead in Charlie's car, was at the same time worrying about her parents and, before they even got to the town, she begged Charlie to stop and turn around. 'I want to tell them,' she said. 'I want to get married with my family around me and everyone friendly. I'm going to tell them that and, if they won't agree, then I'll marry you anyway.'

Charlie was persuaded and he turned the car round and headed back. But he had not travelled far before, rounding a bend, he saw a Romany vardo overturned in a ditch, and then Lisa's father pinned under one of the wagon wheels. Lisa's mother was frantically trying to free him and, as Charlie got out of the car and ran up to her, she cried out to him to help her get her man out. Charlie managed to lever up the wheel and they pulled him out, but it was too late – he was crushed so badly that he died before he reached the hospital.

Lisa and Charlie married shortly afterwards, with her mother present, and then they went to Scotland, to keep away from the rest of the family, who blamed them both for the tragedy. The last that was heard of them was that they were happily married and had seven children.

This is a tale I've heard told many times, sitting round the fire with the women.

Later the men would return and the women would get up and give them bread, cheese, pickles and jugs of ale. The men would take over, singing, dancing and playing instruments long into the night.

ELEVEN

Christmas at the Prison Camp

'Daddy's coming home for a visit,' Mummy said brightly to Nathan and me. He'd sent a telegram and she'd found someone to read it for her. But Nathan was too young to be excited by the news, and I was determined not to build up my hopes this time.

My father was stationed outside London now, at Sunbury, in charge of the cookhouse at a prisoner of war camp. The camp itself was on the Kempton Park racecourse, which now had a thick barbed wire fence all round it and guard towers. Daddy's quarters were situated under the stands. But just outside the main entrance to the course there was a plot of land, the ideal resting place for a caravan! Discipline in the camp was fairly slack, so he decided he could get away with moving us there.

By the winter of 1944 it was generally felt that the war was at last coming to an end, though the south of England was still a target for German bombs. Towards the end of the war, we had these pilotless 'buzz bombs', so-called because of the eerie buzzing noise they would make as they flew overhead. They had inbuilt timing devices, and when the timers ran out, the buzzing would stop and the bomb would fall to the ground, killing anyone and everyone in the near vicinity. People used to fall to the ground when they heard one stop overhead, but by then of course they knew it was too late. I get that same sickening feeling now, in a clairvoyant sense, when I realise I can see something bad in the future but know I can do nothing to change it, for it is already cast.

When he arrived home, Daddy told us to pack our tools – which is how we refer to our vardos and equipment – because he was going to take us with him when he went back. He and my mother talked it over and realised that, with time so short, it was going to be impossible for the horse to haul the vardo all the way to Sunbury and they decided instead to buy a car. Cars were very cheap during the war, since everyone had laid them up.

In fact, the war years completely changed the traveller's way of life. The horse was soon to be a thing of the past as more and more Romanies began to switch to aluminium caravans that could be towed by cars. It probably didn't seem such a drastic step at the time, but we were actually beginning to leave the past and much of our heritage behind.

I remember the journey to Sunbury in the car, which didn't seem to take long at all compared to being pulled by a horse. The journey felt like such a great adventure, especially for us children. When we arrived and pitched the vardo, we must have raised a few eyebrows. It was certainly a strange place to park up and we must have looked an odd sight, our trailer jacked up right in the middle of this little wilderness, just outside the gates of a huge prison camp.

Daddy had told Mummy what she had to say if anyone tried to move us on and, although this was what she expected to happen, it never did. I imagine the army was unsure whether this was part of the property they had taken over, while everyone else assumed the vardo belonged to the army. Obviously no one thought that a Romany family would dare just set up there without permission, but that is exactly what we did and no one bothered us.

In the evening, his duties completed, Daddy would sneak quietly out of the camp and come and stay with us. In fact, he had things very well organised in the camp and seemed to be able to do pretty much what he wanted. He looked after his superior officers well and they, in turn, looked after him. Needless to say, his family did all right as well. There was no shortage of labour, with thousands of prisoners there, and he saw that all our odd jobs were done by them, which they seemed more than pleased to do.

Our water supply was carried over by a young Dutch man. Mummy could vaguely understand why the Germans were held prisoner, but she could not see why the Dutch boy should be. She turned to Daddy one day and said, 'Why should the cheri chore [poor boy] have to be held prisoner, Eddie?'

'Laura,' he said in a condescending tone, 'he's a collaborator.'

He thought he had explained very clearly why the boy should be in prison, but Mummy just looked back at him with a puzzled expression.

'He was due to have been shot for his crimes as a spy. He's better off in a POW camp than dead,' he went on.

Mummy was horrified that this young boy might have been killed. She didn't understand the gorger way of life or what went on in the war. It was all very puzzling to her.

We soon got used to the strange sight of men held captive behind barbed wire and Nathan and I would play on our little patch of land, adjacent to the fence, without taking much notice of it. The men used to smile and wave at us and we would wave back. They were always, all of them, very nice to Mummy and us.

Perhaps, in some way, the sight of children playing cheered them up. In another way, though, I suppose it was a tremendously sad experience for them. It was late December 1944 and the prisoners must have been hoping, desperately, that they would never have to spend another Christmas fenced in like farm animals.

On Christmas Day, I received the most beautiful dolls house I had ever seen. It was absolutely perfect and was fitted out properly, to the tiniest detail, with curtains at the windows and tiny carpets on the floors and furniture, all built precisely to scale. It also had little dolls carved out of wood with arms and legs that actually moved. The prisoners had made it for me. For Nathan, they had made a lovely German sausage dog, a wooden dachshund, with four legs that moved and made it seem to scamper along when pushed; it even had a little wagging tail. We were very happy with our toys, but Mummy was still sad at the injustice of it all, at how wasteful and useless it was that these men should be hemmed in, as she supposed tens of thousands of English prisoners were in Germany. It all seemed so senseless.

Although we had a wonderful Christmas, we were very isolated where we were. Nathan and I would entertain each other, as we didn't have anyone else to play with. One day Mummy came out of the vardo beaming. 'I've made you a telephone,' she announced. This comprised of two tin cans tied together with a piece of string. It was about eight foot long and if I talked into the can, Nathan could hear me by putting his can to his ear. We spent many an hour talking to each other on this fine contraption.

I'm not sure how long we stayed outside the camp. Mummy must have hated it after a while, with no friends or family near and no way to earn a living, and my father was aware that the camp authorities could only turn a blind eye for so long. But before it became an issue, my father was demobbed and we found ourselves on our way back to Lincolnshire.

TWELVE

Pennies from Heaven

'We won the war!' 'The war's over!' Voices were shouting round me, as hundreds of people converged on Spalding's marketplace. I was only six years old so my uncle Nathan hauled me onto his shoulders, my hands tightly gripped in his as I looked over the jostling crowd.

It was 8 May 1945 and Germany had finally surrendered.

A large bonfire had been lit in the middle of the main road and every shop, business and hotel had its doors and windows wide open, lights illuminating the pavements and road. Some people were laughing; others were crying. Children were running around cheering and hooting. Drinks were flowing, but no one wanted to sit in the bars; instead, they spilled out onto the streets, looking for friends and family to celebrate with. The elation of that night stayed with me for a very long time. Mummy was crying with joy and relief, as were the wives and mothers of men away fighting.

It also meant more freedom for us children as our mothers could finally relax without the constant threat of bombing raids. That summer I had not only my cousin Daisy to play with, but also Aunt Lena's daughter Vera, who was the same age as us.

Once our chores were done, we'd be sent out to fetch herbs for our mothers – dandelions to make tea and coffee were top of the list – but we spent most of our time looking for four-leaf clovers.

One day, as we made our way into the fields, Daisy pushed past me shouting, 'Can't catch me, can't catch me! Come on, Eva, come on, Vera. You two are soooo slow.'

Very quickly, she came to a halt. 'Ow!' we heard her shout. I stomached a hearty laugh as I knew exactly what had happened. I'd been out into the field with Mummy the day before and had also been stung, probably by the very same nettles.

'Oh shut up, Eva, it hurts,' she whined, as she hopped from foot to foot, rubbing her legs..

'OK, OK,' I shouted. 'I'll find a dock leaf, hang on.'

Soon I was holding the leaves on her burning skin, and within a matter of seconds you could see her sense of relief as the leaves took away the stinging sensation. During the summer months all three of us would look like we had been in the wars. We were always getting into scrapes and were permanently etched with scars and scratches. That's when Granny's homemade jam would come into its own. Not only was it delicious to eat, but it was also used as medication for our grazed elbows and knees. A jar of jam would always be left open and it would form a fluffy, blue-grey skin, rather like mould mixed with a spider's web. This skin would be placed on the injured part of the body and worked a treat. It's the Romany version of penicillin.

As well as scratches, in early autumn I would always have the itch, because I was allergic to pears and plums and wasn't allowed to eat them. That never stopped me, though. Everyone knew when I'd been bad because I would break out in heat spots, which I would then scratch until my arms and legs were covered in red scabs. These would weep and even then I kept picking the heads off. 'Eva's got the plague again,' Daisy and Vera would chant. But picking the heads off the scabs was something I just couldn't resist, just as I couldn't resist the beautiful plums and pears.

On that particular day, with Daisy covered in nettle stings, we abandoned the idea of looking for four-leaf clovers. 'What next?' Vera asked, deflated, and then we all locked eyes. Grinning, we shouted in unison, 'Mud pies!'

Vera snuck back into her vardo to grab her mother's pudding basin, which she filled with water from the tub outside. Meanwhile, Daisy and I found a spot behind my mother's vardo and started to scoop up earth with our hands until Vera joined us, water sloshing over the sides of the bowl.

An hour later, we were caked with mud and had made three 'chocolate' cakes, four towers and something that resembled a small house, but was now quickly collapsing on the right side. Just as we were about to try to rescue it, a big shadow appeared over us. We froze. Maybe if we pretended we were statues, the shadow would move away. No such luck. A horrified voice shrieked from behind us, 'Daisy, Eva and Vera, look at the state of you all!'

It was our cousin Honour, Daisy's older sister, and she was not pleased. 'Daisy obviously forgot that the dress she is wearing is new, but she's about to remember, aren't you, gal? And as for you two . . .'

I don't know how Honour managed to hold all three of us by our ears at the same time, but somehow she did. We were very quickly and painfully escorted up from the ground and, before I knew it, the pudding basin was being refilled and, along with a torrent of Romany words which I'm sure I should not have recognised at so young an age, we were washed and scrubbed down from head to toe. We were always taught to respect our elders and Honour was three years older than us. At the grand old age of nine, she had an old head on her shoulders.

That is not to say that we were never allowed to make mud pies again. But this was certainly the day we learned never to do it in new clothes!

We were all beautifully clean and tidy for Uncle Nathan's wedding that summer. He was in his mid-forties. Uncle Alger had married in his mid-thirties, but his wife could not take his drinking and by now they had split up, while my uncle Walter never married. Uncle Nathan had fallen in love with Bertha Taylor from Hopton, a very striking Romany girl of about twenty-two, with eyelashes so long they looked like a fringe round her big eyes. The family came from round the country for the traditional ceremony and we had the usual campfire festivities. But Bertha also wanted to be married in a church, in a definite break from tradition for both of the families. She chose St Matthew's church in Lumley Avenue, Skegness.

To this day, I feel guilty and so sorry for poor Bertha. There we were, around twenty children aged from about two to twelve, all of us trouble at the best of times. None of us had been in a church before or had the slightest idea of how to behave. Uncle Cardy had emptied his pockets and given Daisy and me all his pennies, in return for a promise of good behaviour.

We were sat at the back of the church, shuffling a bit on the hard pews, when right in the middle of the ceremony I felt the coins slip out of my hot hand and clatter onto the stone floor. I closed my eyes in horror as the pennies span and then fell flat with an echoing clink. It seemed to last forever. As the church fell silent, I opened my eyes to see rows of faces glaring at me. Even today, I can feel the embarrassment of that moment.

Eventually the vicar coughed and everyone faced forward again as he resumed the service. About five minutes later, Daisy gave me a naughty look, opened her hand and let her pennies fall in a repeat perform-ance. It did make a marvellous noise, but poor Aunt Bertha was nervous as a kitten and the parson was now wondering what the devil was happening.

Daisy and I were in trouble afterwards, but not as much as Uncle Cardy, who got most of the blame for giving us the coins in the first place!

I suppose not having been brought up as church-goers, we did not hold it in much awe. We do believe in God and in right and wrong. As children, it was drummed into us that God did not like wicked people. If I can look in the mirror and know that I have done nothing wrong, haven't deliberately hurt anyone or been unkind, then I can like myself and know God likes me. If I am not ashamed of myself, then God is not ashamed of me. These simple beliefs are widely held by Romanies. We may not practise organised religion, but we would not sin on Saturday and ask for forgiveness on Sunday, as some gorgers seem to do.

When we were children, my father told us that we could go to church if we wished, but he emphasised that he was an atheist, even though my mother was not. In fact, all of my mother's family are very God-fearing people.

Granny managed to get Bertha a kiosk for dukkering at Butlins amusement park and one day my cousin Daisy and I took her a cup of tea. When she'd finished her tea, she asked us to look after the place while she went off to spend a penny.

As soon as she'd gone, I sat down in Bertha's chair and started playing with the crystal ball. This stood on a beautiful black velvet cloth with little silver claws sewn on it which held mock diamonds. Picking idly at these, to see how they were fixed, one of the stones came away in my hand. I was just thinking of how to replace it when a lady put her head inside the door and asked if the clairvoyant was there. We told her that Bertha wouldn't be long and then the lady asked if we had any lucky charms for sale. We had a look around, hating to turn a customer away, but couldn't find any. Then I suddenly remembered the mock diamond I was still clutching. 'Only these,' I said, holding out the stone as though I were offering the Koh-i-noor. 'Sixpence each.'

The lady gave me a funny look, but she gave me the sixpence as well. Daisy and I were in business! She sat plucking the stones out of the black velvet cloth while I stood at the door, calling out, 'Get your lucky charms here! Only a tanner each!' We sold three before Bertha got back.

She never left us in charge again.

THIRTEEN

A Stranger Comes to Stay

'That's the most awful suit I have ever seen in my life,' Mummy said.

'It's OK,' replied Daddy. He was one of the very first men to be demobbed, having done six years' service, and he received eighty pounds as a gratuity and a grey, chalk-striped demob suit which he thought was quite dapper.

With that, Mummy grabbed one of the sleeves of the jacket and clenched it tightly in her fists. She then let go, nodded her head knowingly and said, 'Look at that, all crumpled already. I wouldn't even let you out the door in that. Can you imagine what the arse of your trousers will look like when you've been sitting down for a while?'

They both burst out laughing and within the hour it had been disposed of in the dustbin.

They had been apart more than they had been together during the eight years of their marriage, but now they were free to go back to their own way of life. For Nathan and myself, it was a bit like having a stranger come to stay – this man we hardly knew was now a permanent part of our life. I suppose he must have felt the same way as he seemed reluctant to spend any time alone with us, and definitely didn't tell us stories or play games with us, or do any of the other things a father would normally do with his children. We were in Spalding and continued to make the town our base, but just as my father's return was to change things for us, so the war had changed things forever for the Romany.

There were very few horse-drawn vardos left now, of course, but it was more than that. After the war, things were very different. There was a new kind of outlook. Some of the men had been in the services and had mixed regularly with the gorgers, and the wartime rules and regulations, like rationing, had forced the rest of us into more frequent contact with non-Romanies. More of us were beginning to marry out of the race than ever before.

It wasn't like that for us children, though. We didn't mix with the gorgers more than we had to – and we didn't like playing with the gorger children at all. It was always so boring when they asked us the same questions about our way of life. The main one always being how did we go to the toilet.

Most caravans these days do have toilets built in them, but we would never have dreamed of using an inside toilet. We would have thought it extremely unhygienic, not being able to flush the waste away and carrying it about with you. We used to carry with us a chemical toilet and four sheets of hardboard. As soon as we arrived anywhere, Daddy's first job was to set up the toilet hut and, when we left, he would dispose of the waste in a healthy way, usually by digging a deep hole and covering it with earth, before folding up the hut. We liked to stay in pub yards because they'd have toilets outside. Sometimes, if we were based near some older-type houses, the kind that had their lavatory built at the bottom of the garden, we might make an arrangement with the householder for our family to use that.

As far as rubbish was concerned, we used to carry dustbins around with us and lots of paper bags and sacks. We never, ever littered the countryside and only dumped our rubbish in the places provided by the local authorities. Often we would travel miles in order to take our rubbish to the nearest corporation tip.

We never used public baths, mainly because, though it probably sounds curious to the average gorger, we didn't like the idea of using baths that had been used by other people. We tended to have strip washes all over – and every day, I may add. But we also had a corrugated tin bath that we would use once or twice a week and would fill with water heated in saucepans over the fire. I remember how lovely it felt when the bath water had got cold and Mummy would top it up with a lovely big saucepan of piping hot water. I think the most common misconception about gypsies is that they are dirty, though this probably stems from the fact that so many of us have swarthy skin.

I must admit, though, that there was one thing about the gorger children that fascinated me, and that was the fact that they went to school. From about the age of five, I had a secret determination to learn to read and write. I had a passion for drawing as well, and I knew that at school they drew and painted. Whenever I had the opportunity, I used to ask gorger children questions about what went on at school.

One day, some of them asked if I would like to attend Sunday school with them and, curiosity overcoming my wariness, I asked my mother if I could go. She said she would think about it and, with half an hour still to spare before we needed to head off, I rejoined the gorgers. Eagerly, I asked them all about it: what would it be like, when was playtime? They fell about laughing at me.

'You don't have playtime at Sunday school, silly,' one boy said.

'*You're* silly!' I flared back, feeling hurt and humiliated by their laughter. And then, of course, we started calling each other names and suddenly they were no longer friends but on the other side of the fence, gorger strangers calling me 'stupid gypsy, dirty gypsy' and the rest of their insults. After that incident, I was even more wary of mixing with them.

But the idea of going to school persisted – it was my biggest desire in the whole world. In fact, in a sign of changing times, some travelling people were now sending their children to boarding school in order for them to get an education. It had to be boarding school so that they could continue to travel and earn a living, which was the only way of life they knew.

Mummy told me much later that she'd realised that I had a thirst for knowledge and needed to learn things she couldn't help me with, especially when it came to the three Rs: reading, writing and arithmetic. Just by listening to the radio, she knew how much the world was changing and didn't want me to be left behind. So one Friday morning, she took me to some shops in a little place called Bourne in Lincolnshire and, to my great surprise, asked the man in charge to fit me for a school uniform. My heart nearly stopped with excitement. We left with a beautiful grey jacket and a pleated grey skirt, a white shirt and a white, black and grey tie.

It was unbearable that weekend to wait for Monday

morning. I hardly slept thinking about the fountain of knowledge I was about to encounter. On Monday morning, however, it was a totally different story. I had a panic attack thinking of myself trapped in this school with all of the gorgers. Would I make a fool of myself? Would I get the cane? Would they laugh at me? And, most of all, would they call me a dirty gypsy because I lived in a caravan? With these thoughts in my head, I climbed underneath the table and wrapped myself around one of its legs.

Mummy tried to coax me out with kind words. 'Come on, Eva, this is what you've always wanted.'

'I can't, Mummy, I'm scared.' And, believe me, I was petrified.

However, in the end, my parents got me into the car. 'Do it for me, do what I couldn't,' my mother had said, looking me squarely in the eye, and that had done it.

When we reached the door of the school, my mother asked to see whoever was in charge. A rather tired-looking man sat us in an office, all the while looking at me with puzzlement on his face. Was I already standing out so much? I thought to myself, and the butterflies again began to flutter inside my tummy. He left the room and, within a few moments, one of the largest men I have ever seen in my life entered the office. He had a voice like a foghorn.

'Yes, yes?' he said with urgency and slight irritation in his voice. You could see from the way he was acting that he was a very busy man and we were obviously encroaching on his valuable time. 'How can I help you people?

Mummy explained the situation to him: 'I want my daughter to attend your school.' He had been shuffling his papers into a semblance of order, but now he stopped what he was doing and sat stock-still, staring first at my mother and then at me. The broadest grin washed over his face. 'Let me get this straight,' he said. 'You want your daughter to come to our school?'

My mother stiffened in her seat and I could see that she was ready to challenge anything he said about me not being fit to attend his fancy school. 'We would love to have your daughter come to our school,' he said, now slouching back into his chair. I could see from his demeanour that he was in fact trying to put my mother at ease, not challenge her. There was something in his manner, however, that told me he was also enjoying the situation.

'The only problem I have, or that she might have—,' he started.

'Yes, yes?' my mother asked, with urgency in her voice.

'Is that this, my dear, is an all-boys school.'

With that, the twinkle in my mother's eye returned

and we all burst out laughing, including the headmaster. That was my first and last day at school. I never wore my fancy uniform again.

I didn't give up on my ambition to learn to read and write, though, and my parents never objected, although Daddy didn't have the time or inclination to teach me himself. When they were both away working, they used to hire gorger girls to look after me and I always made them read to me, either comics or the Bible – an odd combination, I know, but these were what I liked to hear. Most of them hated this, especially as I wanted everything explained. They either got absorbed in the comics or bored with the Bible, but whichever way, I was a nuisance to them, not only because they had to read to me, but because I wanted words that I didn't know pointed out to me so that I could learn the outline of their shapes. These shapes I used to copy out laboriously. I had a secret place for all my papers: an old brass coal scuttle with battle scenes embossed on it. This was my own desk where I could keep my personal things.

Sometimes the girls used to try to get out of reading to me. They would rather take me for walks, where they might get the chance to meet a boy. But I would have none of that and, if they didn't do as I wanted and help me learn to read and write, I would threaten to tell stories about them to my mother and get them the sack. I was a little monster, I know, but determined to learn somehow.

They never had to put up with me for too long as we continued to travel around, going wherever we felt might be profitable for us. My father was always trying different businesses and once, when we were near Wisbech, he noticed that the roads were being dug up and tarmacked, the workers discarding the wood blocks that had been used in their original construction. He picked up one of the blocks, out of curiosity, and brought it home to see how well it would burn. It burned beautifully and so, while the supply lasted, we went into the firewood business, my father buying up the whole lot from the council at a dirt-cheap price.

One of our favourite stopping places was in the yard of a pub called the Ship at Boston, a market town surrounded by flat fenland which was near the coast and had a busy port. The pub was set right on the river and I could see the trawlers come in. The fishermen used to keep their gear in the old stables at the back of the Ship and I loved to watch them repairing their nets, their nimble fingers plucking at the net as though it were a musical instrument, the long, sharp needle, shaped like a cheese slice, sparkling and weaving in and out at a fast pace.

We spent a Christmas there when my father rented one of the Ship's stables for a new enterprise. He had learned how to make toys, and with the aid of two pleasant young gorger fishermen, Bob and Jack, turned out hundreds of wooden Mickey Mouse figures, brightly painted and varnished, which he then sold in Boston market.

The two boys were in their early twenties, I suppose, and really nice to me. When they discovered that I was teaching myself to read and write, they helped me and taught me the alphabet in their breaks, which none of the gorger girls who looked after me had ever bothered to do. They also showed me how to join up my letters when writing and during those few weeks over Christmas, I really managed to grasp what it was all about.

Daddy did so well with these toys that we had a very merry Christmas with the proceeds. With my new writing skills, I had carefully inscribed – in very big letters, in case he was short-sighted – our notes to Father Christmas. These had been put on the open fire in the vardo and the ashes had been drawn up the chimney and scattered into the night sky to find their way to the dark and distant land where Father Christmas lived.

As well as new clothes, I received notebooks, pens and pencils to help me with my studies. That was when the family gave me the nickname Bookworm. I was always getting told off for eating and reading at the same time – usually after Nathan had grassed on me!

But I often had to snatch moments when I could sit and learn, as my days were full of other things. As well as my usual chores, by the time the war ended I was being trained in palm-reading and clairvoyance. I'd already gone out with Granny on her calls, mostly to keep me out of the mischief I always seemed to get into, but also so that she could teach me. I could be useful too. There was more than one client who, to put it mildly, was difficult to get away from. While my grandmother was always willing to give help and advice when it was needed, there were some clients who always wanted to prolong the visits, endlessly discussing their problems down to the last detail. Since Granny had no time for this, I would promptly be trotted out as the excuse to leave.

With the war over, the fairgrounds were opening again, so there were plenty of places for us to travel to, and both Granny and my mother had dukkering booths at the amusement park in Skegness. I used to look after the waiting room for my mother, just to make sure no one stole anything or tried to listen to the client ahead of them. I'd also fetch her cups of tea from the café next door, as well as keeping an eye on the girl who was employed to look after Nathan, who seemed to me to be a real little monster. It seems strange, looking back, to think that before too long our roles were reversed and he had to look after me, chaperoning his sister whenever she went out, in the true Romany tradition.

When we were together, Honour would give Daisy, Vera and myself palm-reading sessions. This consisted of learning the lines of the hands and studying the shape, size, colour and texture. We couldn't read each other easily, as we knew what each other wanted and that stood in the way of what we saw. Honour would cover our hands with mud or lipstick and then press them onto paper so that she never knew whose palm she was studying.

As time went on, the clairvoyant sense inside me continued to develop, even though I was unaware of it. Sometimes, while with my grandmother, I would say things like, 'Mummy wants me to get her some tea from the café,' or 'I'd better go now because Mummy wants to go home,' quite without thinking. It never occurred to me to ask myself how I knew these things. I just knew.

I used to study the clients, even at a young age, and ask my mother questions like 'Why is that lady going to hospital?' or 'Will they be all right when they go to Australia?' without ever knowing why I did. This may sound rather weird, but it is accepted in Romany life. Nobody patted me on the head and told me what a clever little girl I was.

I was seven years old when I was first asked to make a prediction for a client. We were at an air show and several of the young airmen came into the caravan where my mother was giving readings. There was one young man who asked my mother if the kid who was looking at him could read hands. 'Come on,' he said, 'tell me what you see, kid!'

I looked down into his hands with interest, trying to seem as mature and serious as possible. The next thing I knew, my stomach turned over and I felt sick and dizzy. I ran out of the caravan as fast as I could and hid.

The next day one of the other airmen came to see my mother and quietly told her that the pilot had been killed.

FOURTEEN

The Coldest Winter

I remember the beginning of 1947 vividly. It was a long, harsh winter. If I breathed hard enough against the vardo window, I could melt the snow that had drifted across it, look outside and see the world all white and still. We were in the yard of the Ship at Boston, a regular stopping place for my family when we were in the area. We had arrived just in time, before the deep snow came.

Within days, we were cut off from the town by drifts more than three feet in depth which blocked the roads and marooned all traffic. The reflection from the white carpet of snow was bright enough to hurt the eyes. The only relief was the steel grey of the sky above it. The milkman who supplied the pub would leave our milk outside the vardo and when I'd open the door to bring the bottles in, I'd see the cream on top had frozen, expanded and pushed through the cardboard bottletop. One of my perks was to eat this delicious ice cream.

Gorgers who live in houses have no idea of the comforts of a vardo, which can be warm and cosy in the hardest of weather, as there aren't a dozen doors and twice as many windows through which the winds can creep, no floorboards or skirtings to let in the draughts, no brick walls for damp to rise up, nor slates that can leak. We were warm as toast for the first few days after the snow settled.

My parents were worried, though, for no one had forecast that the weather would turn as vicious as it had. Outside, it may have been as pretty as a picture on a Christmas card, but the yard tap had frozen solid and was unusable. The pub's taps had frozen too and my father helped the landlord lag the pipes to get the water trickling through them again.

So far as fuel for the stove was concerned, we only carried enough to last us for a few days at a time, especially when on the move, for the lighter our burden the better. Our lighting was supplied by Calor gas, which also fuelled the oven. We normally kept the Calor gas tank outside, for safety, but that particular winter it froze up and my father had to bring it inside the vardo. The level of gas was low, with no more than six hours' left.

If the gas ran out, we could cook on top of the stove and use candles for lighting, but we only had a bucketful of anthracite left. It was impossible to beg, borrow or buy fuel from anyone because the bad weather had set in so suddenly that everyone had been caught out. If anyone had laid in a good stock of fuel, they were certainly not admitting it.

Because of the deep drifts, there were no deliveries to the town and none were made out of it. We were clothed warmly enough, though, and the big pot of stew which my mother kept going all the time on top of the stove made sure that we were kept warm from the inside as well. We must have been there for about five days. The people from the public house kept us supplied with provisions, but both my parents knew that these supplies would begin to dwindle if the weather didn't change.

The nearest coal yard was more than two miles away and the road to it was iced over and not only undriveable, but also practically unwalkable. But my father knew that he had to make the journey somehow. So over his normal winter clothes, he put on an extra pair of socks and another thick pullover. He never wore gloves and so did not have any. My mother tried to get him to wear a pair of hers, but they just wouldn't fit. So, with his hands in the pockets of his Crombie overcoat, he went out into the freezing cold, smiling cheerfully to us as he went through the gate that led to the road.

I stayed by the window, expecting him back any moment. My mother, who knew it would be a hard journey for him, tried to get me interested in my books and pencils, or the new jigsaw puzzle they had bought for me, but I refused to leave my place. It seemed as though I waited for hours and hours and indeed it must have been that long, for the bright snow dulled as grey as the sky and darkness crept in. When it started to snow again, Mummy joined me at the window and we took turns to rub away the steam caused by our breath, watching through the finger-smeared glass for a figure at the gate which was now just a grey shadow we could hardly make out.

There was only a glimmer of light left when we saw a hunchbacked figure appear in the distance. He was doubled over with the weight of a whole sack of coke on his back and he approached the caravan at a snail's pace. My mother ran out and dragged him into the caravan, sack and all, for the two could not be parted; the sack was frozen to his hands and he couldn't let it go.

The kettle had been kept on and off the boil for hours, ready to make him mugs of steaming hot tea on his return, and my mother poured the hot water onto a towel and massaged his hands with it, so he could pull them away from the neck of the sack. His face was absolutely grey, his eyes closed, there was snow on his eyelashes and his eyebrows and his hair; he looked like an old, old man.

He couldn't move to help himself and she had to struggle to get him out of his overcoat, then sit him down and pull off his shoes and socks. She stuck his feet in a bowl of hot water and, as he slowly warmed to life, she ran across to the pub to get him some brandy. With a good measure of that inside him, and about half a gallon of hot tea, he came back to something like normal again, but he had a hot ache in his feet and hands which stayed with him for some time afterwards.

We learned a big lesson from that winter and never again, no matter how troublesome it was to carry, did we let ourselves run short of fuel. Because, even with the sack of coke for the stove, we still had a problem to solve, with no Calor gas for lighting. My parents both agreed, though, that it would do until tomorrow.

When the next day arrived, it was just as bad, worse if anything, for the snow had drifted down all night. It was deep enough for five-year-old Nathan to disappear in it, and knee-deep for a tall adult. My father ploughed a furrow through to the pub and, from there, phoned all the depots, sites, boat yards, anywhere and everywhere he could think of that might keep a supply of Calor gas. He had no luck. They were all out of stock and not expecting any more supplies until traffic could get through again.

He came back to the vardo, put on all his winter

clothes again and went out, swearing that he wouldn't return until he'd got some from somewhere. He was headed for the river and, in the mood he was in, I think we were quite worried that he meant to drown himself if he didn't find his gas.

But a number of cabin cruisers were moored on the river and my father guessed most of these would have facilities that were much the same as we had in the vardo. He was right in his guess and there, in full view, just inside the cabin of one of the boats, was a large cylinder that had clearly hardly been used. My father explained his problem to the man who looked after the craft and the man said he was sorry, but under no circumstances could he let anything be taken off any of the boats without the owners' permission. So then my father asked who owned that particular boat and, fortunately, it was a local man who lived not too far away – although in that weather even a short distance seemed miles. He went up to see the man, but he was away in the South of France, according to the house-keeper. She too was sympathetic, but refused to act without permission, so he was stuck again.

By this time, the best of the day, such as it was, had already gone and he knew that if he had to visit the owner of each boat that might have gas aboard it could take a week. So he went back to the river, waited until the boatman went off for a break, then forced open the door of the cabin cruiser and removed the gas cylinder. He left a note for the owner, explaining exactly what he'd done and why he'd done it and that he would leave the money with the governor at the pub. He then fixed the lock so that it would be secure again and went off with his prize.

My father, for all his many faults, would never steal. He didn't believe in it, and neither do I. And I think the man whose boat it was must have acknowledged and respected that about him because he never did attempt to collect his money from the landlord at the pub. I think he knew just how desperate my father must have been feeling at that time.

So we had warmth and light, and a few days after that the weather did finally break and start to clear. Mummy would come up with different ideas to keep us occupied, from cleaning and polishing the silver to cutting up my comics and making shapes with them. We played I Spy and, of course, we had the radio and listened to *Down My Way* and *Workers' Playtime*, and Tommy Handley and Jack Train in *It's That Man Again*. She also taught Nathan and me how to waltz and do the quickstep. Both Mummy and I had a battle on our hands when Nathan kept insisting on opening the door to try to get out and play in the snow. A couple of times, we were both allowed out, but after just a few minutes we'd run back into the vardo, covered with snow, with a hot ache in our fingers and toes. Hot milk and toast with jam would warm our insides and get us feeling right as rain again in no time.

Eventually, after being stuck and out of work for some weeks, the snow melted and we got on the road again, this time to Stamford, about forty miles away, where their annual mid-Lent fair was due to be held in a couple of days' time. Traffic was heavy and it took us ages to get there, but eventually we did and parked on a large piece of waste ground which sloped down to the River Welland (which flowed through Spalding too, on its way to the sea). The river was running high with melted snow. We were parked by the recreation ground, where part of the fair would be held, alongside the wagons of the fairground travellers.

It was the usual pattern on that night. The men went off to the local and the women whom we knew from previous fairs came round to our vardo and swapped tales of the hardships endured during the spell of bad weather.

We children were in bed, but I was still awake when my father came in at about ten o'clock. He must have been exhausted, for there had been all the packing up when we'd left that morning, and then the dead-slow crawl all the way to Stamford in terrible conditions, and then getting parked and jacked up on the new site. Wanting nothing more than to drop right into bed and off to sleep, he was aghast when my mother told him that she wanted him to move the wagon there and then.

'What are you talking about, woman?' he demanded. 'I'm hungry. Come on, let's have a meal and get to bed.'

I sat up, taking all of this in. 'Eddie,' replied my mother, 'I am absolutely serious. The river is going to come up tonight and we are going to be flooded, and we can't stand any more expense or trouble.'

'Look,' my father said, very patiently under the circumstances, 'I've just been talking in the pub with some men from the river boards and it so happens I made a point of asking them if there was any danger of flooding and they said there was no chance.'

'I don't care what they said,' my mother answered back, and then one thing led to another and it finished up a right old row. But no matter how much my father complained, she just would not give in. So, in the end, swearing under his breath, he went outside to get on with the job. It is no easy task to move a vardo. He had to pack all the gear inside, then get the motor in position to tow the caravan, then wind up the jacks, which were placed at the four corners. But at last he was ready to go.

He started up the motor, which promptly died on him. He tinkered about with it for about a quarter of an hour, the metal freezing cold on his hands, cursing his bad luck. Then he realised he was out of petrol and that was the last straw. He slammed into the vardo and announced that he would put up the jacks again and we would move in the morning.

'If we don't move now,' said my mother, 'I am going to take these children and book into a hotel,' and she started to get us out of bed and dressed. Realising she was never going to change her mind, my father went off to a neighbour's wagon and asked if he could borrow some petrol. They thought he was mad to move anywhere that night, but lent him the petrol and, after some fuss and bother, he managed to get the car started. By this time it was nearly midnight and all our neighbours, and their neighbours, had come out to see what the noise and fuss was all about.

The travelling men thought it was a big joke, my father moving at that time of night, just because his woman said he had to, and my father was well aware that he was something of a laughing stock.

To make matters worse, he still couldn't get moving, because the churned-up ground had turned to thick mud and the motor wheels could not get a grip. So the men had to give him a push, while he steered, practically all the way up the hill, to the level ground at the top, with the wheels slipping every few yards. We made it at last, accompanied by cheers, and as we got our vardo jacked up again, we could hear the men's laughter as they went back down the hill to their own caravans, calling out mocking goodnights to us. My father, tight-lipped, said nothing. He refused the meal my mother offered him and, completely worn out, went straight to bed as soon as we were all settled.

The next day, when we looked out of the window, it was like looking down on a lake. There had been heavy rain in the night and the river had burst its banks. The whole of the site was flooded to a depth of two or three feet. Portable lavatories, buckets, bowls, equipment, all the gear that would normally be kept outside was floating everywhere.

My mother didn't say a word other than that she was going to help, and she waded in with the other women and helped them to salvage what goods they could. I clearly remember my father saying to me, though I was only a child, 'She's always doing things like this and she's always damn well right, bloody woman. She's marvellous and I don't know why I argued with her. I suppose it was because I was so tired.'

This, and many other incidents like it, gave all of us a healthy respect for my mother's clairvoyant powers – although we thought of it more as good judgement than anything mystical. If our feelings tell us to act a certain way, we Romanies listen to them, especially when it comes to the well-being of the family, the most important thing to us. We children certainly learned not to question Mummy as, in our minds at least, there was no one wiser than her.

FIFTEEN

Up with the Turkey, Down with the Mirror

Mummy had arranged with Aunt Vera to spend Christmas 1947 in Wisbech, behind a pub called the Dun Cow, whose landlord, Dick Barton, had agreed we could stay in his car park. He but was very fond of our family and looked upon us as friends – Uncle Cardy in particular. I was in awe of him because I believed he was the very same 'Dick Barton, Special Agent' whose adventures we listened to on the radio!

Our Romany Christmases were much like those of the gorgers, I suppose. We had our turkey, which we cooked in our Calor gas oven, and a Christmas pudding. We didn't use holly as a decoration, though, for that was considered unlucky. And we listened with interest to the King's speech on the radio.

That Christmas, my father was sent shopping on his own in our car, with instructions from my mother on what and what not to buy. He came back from town and unloaded vast amounts of shopping, mostly food, and I went to see if I could help. I opened the boot and saw a beautiful red bicycle inside, exactly what Nathan had asked for in the letter I had written for him to Father Christmas.

It was the first moment that I had any doubt about there being a real Father Christmas, and it was heart-breaking. I remember thinking, desperately trying to come up with excuses, that perhaps our parents did not know what Nathan had asked for and he would have two red bicycles on Christmas Day. But in my heart, I had guessed the truth. I slammed down the lid of the boot, looking around to see if anyone had seen me, and then went back to the caravan, pretending I didn't know.

Sure enough, there was only one bike laid at the foot of Nathan's bed on Christmas morning. I had asked for a wristwatch and that was there too, but suddenly the magic had completely gone out of Christmas. Later that day, I talked the whole thing over with Vera, who also had her suspicions. We agreed that my discovery proved the point: there was no Father Christmas. All these years, we had been tricked!

We both went to my mother and asked her point blank. I think she knew I had found out because she made no attempt to cover up. She explained to us in simple words that it was the spirit of Christmas which was the truth and which was important, not the various legends surrounding it. And she made us feel very important by telling us that, now we were grown up and knew about these things, it would be up to us to keep the younger children as excited and happy as we had always been waiting for Father Christmas to visit us.

Soothed by her words, I was able to go outside and enjoy Christmas with all the other children, even though Vera and I exchanged a few knowing, grown-up glances at the antics of Nathan and Vera's little sisters Lavinia and Dixie and their tales of what Santa Claus had brought them. There is not much room in a traveller's wagon for children to play with their toys and so, however cold it is, any Romany site on Christmas Day is a mass of new, shiny toys and hordes of kids showing them off to each other, swapping them and shouting with excitement.

Most nights the men would adjourn to the public house while the children were being put to bed, but on Christmas Eve, as it was a special time, Aunt Vera and Mummy decided to go to the pub and get crisps and lemonade for the children and a couple of bottles of Guinness for themselves.

At the pub, the landlady insisted they should have a drink with her, and so they had a cherry brandy each.

Then they felt it would be impolite not to buy the land-lady a drink in return, and so they had another cherry brandy. And so on, until an hour and a half later, mindful that the men were waiting for them so they could go out, they returned to the vardos, full of good spirits in every sense. I remember my father pacing up and down, getting angrier and angrier. I was thinking to myself, he goes to the pub every night and Mummy never does.

The waiting men were by then not exactly in the best of tempers and when my mother and Aunt Vera did return, breathing cherry-brandy fumes, the words flowed fast and the language was picturesque. My father forbade my mother to come in and locked the door of the vardo to prevent her. This probably amused the men, but it didn't amuse my mother. If he didn't open the door, she warned, she would put a brick through a window. Which she did! A brick through one of the glass windows of our brand-new, uninsured caravan!

The door was hastily opened but, by now, my mother's blood was really up. She stormed into the vardo, picked up the turkey, which was our Christmas dinner for the next day, and heaved it straight at the beautiful mirror which stood above the fireplace, shattering it. With a window broken, it turned out to be a freezing cold night. It needed to be, to cool that raging hot temper. We learned that Uncle Cardy had been so angry that Aunt Vera had been drinking that he put his foot through the table.

Next day, they were all friends again. Everyone laughed at what had gone on, we children especially, and we made up a song for ourselves: 'Up with the Turkey, Down with the Mirror, on with the Fight' to the tune of 'Start the Day Right'. Even now, when we have a family get-together, we remind ourselves of that day by singing the turkey song.

Aunt Vera had a client in Wisbech who was a good knitter and Vera asked her to knit an outfit for a dolly that she had bought for Daisy. She had also bought one for me and given it to Mummy. Just before Christmas, the lady brought the outfit down and Mummy said to her, 'I'd love one of those outfits for Eva's doll. Could you please make me one?' The woman agreed and, on Christmas Eve, she brought it to our vardo and discreetly handed it over.

The next day, at the foot of our beds, were these beautiful dolls in their lovely outfits. They were the same, except for the fact that Daisy's was pink and mine was bright red. We were walking around the site with our dollies, thinking of names for them, when I decided I wanted to go to the toilet. There was a nice clean toilet outside the pub in the yard, one of the reasons, in fact, that we used to stay there. I asked Daisy to hold my dolly while I went in and she agreed.

But when I came out, my doll was lying in a pool of muddy water.

'I'm so sorry, Eva, I just dropped it,' exclaimed Daisy. 'I didn't mean to!' My beautiful doll was ruined. I picked her up, the tears rolling down my face.

'Don't worry, it will wash off and be good as new,' Daisy said, trying to comfort me.

Aunt Vera took the doll from my hands and brightly said, 'It looks like your baby likes playing in the mud, just like you used to.' That coaxed a watery laugh out of me. 'Come with me and watch me clean her up. And I've got some sweeties in my vardo.'

When we were in our twenties, Daisy took me to one side and admitted she'd deliberately dropped my doll in the mud because she was jealous of the red outfit. She had obviously had this on her conscience for a long time!

SIXTEEN

Bombsites and Babies

We had mainly travelled around Lincolnshire in the first couple of years after my father's return and Mummy was desperate to get back to Spalding to be near the family again. But in 1948 my father wanted to see what other parts of the country were like. So, with Mummy's feelings pushed to one side for my father's, we made our way to the Midlands and found ourselves in Coventry, the city of the three spires. It must have been a beautiful place before the bombings. There were still elegant buildings, but few of them were whole. Mostly, they draped like torn fabric, ragged and blackened at the edges. Great gaping holes torn by the bombs gave the city a toothless smile.

Some of the travellers had told my parents that there was a piece of ground, known as the bombsite, where they were allowed to pull in. The ruins of the bombed buildings had been cleared away and levelled off and a few travelling people had discovered this to be a useful caravan park. The city council let them stay there, which was common sense, as the ravaged land was not much use for anything else.

Over on the other side of the bombsite, away from the vardos, there were lots of bushes, plants and flowers, including lupins of a glorious pinky-purple colour and rosebay willowherb, which was nicknamed bombweed in those days, as it seemed to be the first plant to return to the bombsites. There were also raspberry bushes, from which we would later gather the fruit to make jam. There must have originally been a concreted area, because there was a lot of broken concrete and long grass, as well as a huge hole in the ground which was now a pond and had obviously been made by a bomb. There were also hundreds of frogs and grasshoppers in the long grass – horrible little things. They were everywhere. All you could hear all day and night was that buzzing noise they make. The main sights I remember were the ladybirds and the large number of beautiful butterflies. There must have been about ten different varieties, including Red Admirals, Painted Ladies and Clouded Yellows. Their velvet-like wings had beautiful colours and patterns, and I would watch them fluttering about for hours. Nathan would catch the grasshoppers and put them in a jar, but, however much I hated them, I would insist that he let them out. We would have terrible fights about this because he wanted to take them back to the caravan, which neither Mummy nor I approved of.

I was nine years old and had no idea that my mother was about to give birth, or even that she was pregnant! Pregnancy was not something Romany women would discuss openly, and certainly not with children. Apparently, the plan had been that we would travel to Skegness to be near the family for 'the event', but she could feel that her time was near and that she wouldn't be able to make the journey. So the bomb-site it was!

There was a couple living in a vardo quite near us. He was a businessman, she was an ex-dancer. From an early age, my mother had taught me to tap dance. Every day we would practise the steps she had taught me and work out various routines. One day the lady saw me practising on a tap board outside our caravan. 'She's not bad,' she remarked to Mummy. 'My name is Ellen. I used to be a dancer in shows in London. Why don't I put her through her paces?'

Mummy agreed, and I had a whale of a time learning new steps and routines with her, things like the sailor's hornpipe that I'd never even heard of before.

As it got nearer to Mummy's time to have the baby, Ellen said, 'Shall I come and do some cleaning for you? I love cleaning.'

My mother gratefully agreed and took her on, but

insisted that she pay her. The next morning Ellen turned up and Mummy, Nathan and I left her to it and went off into town to buy Nathan and myself a new pair of shoes each. Mummy bought me a beautiful pair of red tap shoes and I couldn't wait to get home to try them out.

When we got back to the vardo, everything was absolutely gleaming, but the reek of paraffin was overwhelming. Dumbfounded, Mummy questioned Ellen about the smell.

'Paraffin's the best cleaner in the world,' Ellen said.

We could barely step inside the vardo without holding our hands over our noses. That evening, with all the windows and doors open, we spent almost the entire night cleaning the wagon all over again, trying to get rid of the smell. After that, Ellen's nickname became Madam Paraffin and she was only allowed to give me tap lessons. No more cleaning!

Mummy hadn't seen a doctor throughout her pregnancy, so didn't have a date around which she expected to deliver the baby. About three weeks after the paraffin incident her contractions began, at 9 p.m. on the evening of 22 May. She grabbed my arm and said very quietly but firmly, 'Go to the pub on the corner immediately, gal, and get your father.'

I knew from Mummy's tone that something important was happening, and I have never run so fast in my whole life. When my father came back, there were hushed conversations. I suppose Mummy must have known that her labour was in the early stages. The next morning my father took us off for Sunday lunch at the house of Mr and Mrs Lyons, who he'd met in the pub. I certainly didn't want to go, and neither did Nathan. This was most unusual and we really didn't have a clue what was actually going on.

When we got there, Mrs Lyons had prepared the most disgusting food and her house was dirty. How could Mummy let me come here? I thought. And why were Nathan and I being sent here alone?

Mrs Lyons, a fat and matronly looking woman, dipped a comb into a bowl in the sink which had potatoes and cabbage in it, scooped it through the dirty water and then combed her long, greasy grey hair with it. Oh my God, this woman was going to make us eat the food which she had just infected with her dirty comb! I watched as long grey hairs floated to the top of the bowl and my stomach turned over.

How could my parents send us here? I would rather have cooked for us at home. When Daddy came back to pick us up, it had seemed like days rather than hours. He drove us home in silence, but all the time with a wry smile on his face. When we arrived, the wagon was dark and quiet and all of the curtains had been shut.

'Now listen, you two,' whispered Daddy. 'Mummy hasn't been feeling very well. The doctor has been and said it's because she needs another baby. He brought two babies for you to choose from. Which one do you want?'

All of a sudden, a wail came from next to Mummy. I rushed over to see two little bundles, swaddled in white flannelette sheets.

'Oh Mummy,' I said. I could feel the tears welling up. I loved babies and couldn't believe my eyes. 'However are we supposed to choose?'

Little did I know that my mother had been expecting a baby for nine months. Little did my mother know that what she thought was only one baby was in fact two! My sister Anne was born around lunchtime on this warm May day and two hours later, to Mummy's and the midwife's surprise, out came Eddie, feet first!

'Come on, choose then, Eva,' demanded Daddy. I looked at the two small bundles and my heart melted. I was overcome with emotion and the love poured out of me for them both. How could I ever choose between them? It was all too much. I ran out of the wagon sobbing and threw myself on the ground. It was too cruel to have to make this decision.

I heard movement at the vardo door and picked myself up. I was hysterical. 'You're not taking them! You're not taking them!'

My mother managed to lift herself out of the bed. 'Enough, Eddie, stop teasing the girl. Can't you see she's upset? This game has gone on long enough.'

Mummy came over to me and gathered me up in her arms. She walked me back into the vardo and gently pushed me down onto the bed, next to the two babies. She placed the little boy in my arms and whispered gently, 'Daddy's just joking. They're both ours. Do you want to help me look after them?'

I looked down and I swear he winked at me. I placed my finger in his hand. Immediately he grasped it and at that moment I felt so proud and protective of him. Mummy picked up the girl and said, 'We're going to call this one Anne. What do you think? The little boy is Eddie, after your father.'

Months later, I was to be a little upset that these two babies were given names straight away, as they told me I had been called 'it' for three weeks!

So now we were a family of six. The vardo suddenly became a very small place to live indeed, especially as Mummy had decided she wanted a big twin Silver Cross pram for her new babies, as well as two separate cots. There was only one thing to do: it was time to buy a bigger wagon. After much searching around and head-scratching, Mummy came up with an idea. We couldn't tow two wagons easily, but we could buy a bigger vehicle to tow the wagon and store the prams and so on. 'Let's buy a bus!'

When she told my father her idea, he almost choked on the tea he was drinking. 'A bus? Are you mad, woman?'

'I'm very serious,' said Mummy. 'And Mr Blake, who's a millionaire, has got one which he tows his wagon with. If it's good enough for him . . .'

They'd encountered Mr Blake a few times while travelling, and Mummy must have been taken with his bus, which was painted battleship grey and had leaded windows – it looked like a little cottage on wheels. Within a couple of days, Daddy drove up with a Leyland bus, which he proceeded to have stripped out and lined with wood and Formica. He hired a professional carpenter and spent almost every penny they had on his new project.

Shortly after the twins were born, Mummy bought her new Silver Cross pram. It was a nice day, so she decided to take us all for a walk to try it out. When we got back to our vardo, she suddenly said to me, 'In that shop we passed there were some juicy-looking oranges in the window. Go and get them and we'll sit outside and eat them.'

Nathan and I ran to the shops together. I could almost taste the juice of the delectable oranges in my mouth as we ran. I passed the money over to the lady behind the counter. 'As many of those oranges in the window as I can have for half a crown please.' She went to the window with a brown paper bag and came back and handed the bag to me. Nathan and I ran back to the vardo.

When we got back, Mummy grabbed the bag. 'Right, outside, everybody,' she smiled. Her beaming smile turned into a scowl when she looked into the bag.

'What's wrong, Mummy?' I said.

'These are not the oranges in the window,' she exclaimed with surprise and a look of disappointment. 'These are all shrivelled up. Right, come on then, let's go back to the shop.'

We stood in the doorway. 'Hang on to the pram, Eva,' she instructed me and she went into the shop. The woman behind the counter saw her coming and obviously knew what the problem was.

'I'm not taking them back,' she shouted. 'You dirty gypsies live in a caravan and you've been touching them!'

With that, my mother seemed to relax. She smiled and said, 'Oh, but you *are* having them back.' And then she started throwing the oranges. She was hitting the cans on the shelves behind the woman and Nathan and I started to laugh. The nasty woman was ducking and diving.

When Mummy had thrown the last one, we headed

back to the caravan. Mummy had tears rolling down her cheeks from laughter and said, 'It was worth half a crown; I haven't enjoyed myself so much for a long time. We won't use that shop again!'

The bread man was much nicer and Nathan and I would wait eagerly for his van to pull up on the site every morning at around ten o'clock. Mummy would always give her order to us and we would go out and tell him what she wanted. Then we would say, 'What cakes have you got please?' Every morning he would go through the same routine. 'I've got jam tarts, Eccles cakes, iced buns, strawberry tarts, macaroons, chocolate cakes, custard tarts, custard slices, chocolate éclairs, doughnuts, cream meringues and lemon curd tarts.' It was, of course, a game with us. We knew all too well what he had, we just liked to hear him say it, and he knew this too because we always used to end up ordering the same thing: custard tarts! But he played the game, God love him. Mummy would have killed us if she'd known that we were teasing him so badly every day.

By now my parents were beginning to run low on funds. They had only been expecting one baby, after all, and Mummy hadn't been able to get back out to work yet with twins to look after. Add on the cost of a pram, a bus and furnishings and it was clear that they had to start getting some more money coming in.

The *World's Fair*, a newspaper which advertises markets and fairs and acts as a notice board for funerals, weddings and getting in contact with other travelling people, was my parents' first port of call. By scouring the pages, they learned to their delight that Hearsall Common, on the outskirts of Coventry, was having its annual fair the following week. Mummy was confident that if the tobermush (the boss of the fairground) would let them on, she could earn some money again.

Although we weren't bona fide members of the Showmen's Guild, the tobermush would let us have a pitch if we paid him a decent rent. We pulled into the tober (fairground) at Hearsall Common and were allocated a place next to a man rattling cases of bottles as he set up his lemonade stall. 'Lemon, lime and orange,' he'd call. 'Come and get your lovely lemon, lime and orange.' Behind him was a row of swinging boats, gaily painted yellow and trimmed with green, red and blue. The husband and wife proprietors were busy setting them up. The wife, an elderly, plump, blonde lady, was hammering bolts through the framework while her husband secured the nuts. On the other side was a darts stall.

Everywhere there was tremendous bustle and excitement, the sound of generators chugging away and the bitter smell of diesel oil, as the travellers erected their stalls and side shows, assisted by their pinafored women, curlers peeping out from beneath their head-scarves.

What a different picture the fair presented at night, though, when the fairground was alive with people and the hurdy-gurdy sounds mingled with the latest pop records and the giant wheel turned and everything was a splash of colour. It was at that time of day that those mousy traveller wives looked like so many film stars, with their hair now perfectly set and their faces beautifully made up, dressed to kill. They were as much a part of the decoration as the painted scrolls on the roundabouts or the dazzling lights; they helped build up the gay, garish spectacle that is the fairground and that enchants us all.

I still remember the beautiful floaty dress Mummy wore on the first night as she stood out so much from the rest of the women. There was just always something about her, and it was that something that made her who she was. She seemed to float around the fairground that evening, taking in the colours, the smells and the sights around her. She felt as though she'd come home again, as she was never more at ease than when she had set up shop and was watching the familiar sights of the other travellers selling their wares and rides and making their living, just as she was hers.

The women travellers work every bit as hard as

their menfolk, not only during the show, but when setting up as well – building their stalls, painting their caravans, lugging huge cans of water and heavy pieces of equipment which would make the average woman faint just to think about. In the fairground world, everyone mucks in, including the children. It is the system – one for all and all for one – a kind of extension of the Romany family idea, and is why the fairground is the one place outside our own camping ground and family where we can feel at home and can live side by side with the gorgers, because all fairground people have a similar idea about life.

Just as she looked forward to meeting her Romany family and friends on the road, exchanging information about who was doing what, so she did with the travellers. Not all of them stay together from fair to fair; they split up, as Romanies do, and go their own way. So when they arrive at a new fair it is a time to meet up with old acquaintances. Mummy knew many of the people at Hearsall Common and met many more who would become firm friends.

She kept Nathan and me busy picking up the litter around the wagon, cleaning the windows and generally helping out. I also had to keep an eye on all the other travelling children. Around six o'clock on the first evening, before it got really dark, she sent Nathan and me for a stroll around. She knew how curious I would be – just as curious as she had been at the same age. The fair wasn't fully underway at that hour and she knew that all of the stallholders had a strict under- standing to keep an eye on each other's children.

The fairground was great and Nathan and I loved the throb of the generators. They seemed to create a sense of excitement inside us as we picked our way over the heavy cables that ran from them and were hitched up to the rides and lighted stalls, or joints as we used to call them. The smell of the diesel oil mingled with the tempting smell of candy floss, toffee apples and hot dogs with onions. And, of course, there was the music: Guy Mitchell singing 'She Wears Red Feathers', Johnnie Ray belting out 'Cry'.

One of the show people touted at Nathan and me. 'Come on, love, try your luck at Fishing for Ducks.'

'Traveller,' I shouted back, feeling very grown up to use the password that showed I wasn't an outsider. The rosy-faced woman on the stall just winked at us. 'I know, love, I know. I'm just playing with you.' She called us over and let us play on her stall while she waited for the evening bustle to get underway. What we were really doing, of course, was 'geeing' for the lady – pretending to be a customer having a go at the stall and then standing holding a big prize, as though we had won it. It is a time-honoured way of creating a crowd.

As we made our way around the stalls, we also agreed to gee for a girl on the hoopla stall and got talking to her. Nathan, who was rather good at it, managed to get a hoop over a plinth which had a sparkling watch on top, as a prize. We hadn't paid for the games and weren't entitled to anything, but six-year-old Nathan, of course, didn't understand this. He started screaming blue murder because he wanted the watch he thought he had won and I had to try to explain to him. The girl in charge was very kind and understanding and even offered him a rubber ball for his efforts, but this only served to make him scream even more.

I apologised, explaining that he must be tired, and somehow managed to drag him home, clutching the rubber ball that he'd screamed he didn't want. After that I refused to let him go near any more stalls because of the way he had shown me up. I pushed him into the vardo, where Mummy told me to wash his hands and face before dinner, after which we were both promptly told to go to bed for embarrassing our parents. I had never really protested against my parents' discipline before, but on this particular evening I thought it was far too unfair to punish me for something Nathan had done. Besides, I'd been having so much fun and was so excited by the buzz of the fair that there was no way I could have gone to sleep then. I was fed up with the injustice of it all.

'I'm older than he is,' I said crossly, 'and I don't want to go to bed yet. Why should I?'

Almost to my surprise, no one fought me. 'All right then,' said Mummy. 'Put Nathan to bed and you can stay up for a bit.' Hardly able to believe my good fortune, I revelled in my new-found responsibility. I was nine years old, but I felt like the most grown-up person in the world.

The fair lasted several days and we all enjoyed ourselves, for the weather stayed fine, business for Mummy was bustling and money was rolling in at last. Daddy took up the Aptus camera and was snapping away, strolling around the fair looking for customers for his pictures while Mummy was busy dukkering. At the end of it all, they were more than a little pleased with their profits.

While Mummy was giving readings, as usual I would sit in and learn from her. Getting customers to relax is an art in itself, for usually they are petrified, and often their palms will be sweaty, which is why we don't always touch their hands, but use something like a chopstick or a pen to avoid picking up any germs. I would sit watching my mother work in awe and would try to test myself, to see if I could come to the same conclusions as she did. Sometimes clients seem to assume that they have to sit down and tell you all their problems, so getting them to shut up is another art. I was taught by Mummy early on that before they can get their bum on the seat and start talking, you just say, in a loud voice, 'Now, I'm going to tell you what I see and what I feel'.

Mummy loved the fair – the sound of laughter and people enjoying themselves. It reminded her of the good times she'd had with her sisters and the laughter they used to share. She was a different person with her sisters, lighter, freer, always laughing. I know she wanted that for her own children, but Daddy seemed determined to keep us separate from her people.

Now that they had lined their pockets and could be sure they had money for food and other essentials, Mummy was looking forward to joining up with her family and showing off her new twins. Little did she know that her husband had other ideas.

Daddy had disappeared from the fairground one day and had not told Mummy where he had been and what he had been doing. I had been left with the job of looking after the twins and Nathan as usual, and the past few days had been too busy for Mummy to think of anything but working, cooking dinner and then getting her and us children to bed, ready for the next busy day. However, now that their work here was done, she realised that she had no idea what her husband had been up to. She was about to find out, and it was not something she would be happy about.

Daddy walked into the wagon, beaming from head to toe. Mummy knew this smug look and swallowed hard before saying to him, 'What have you done now?'

'I've bought a shop in the middle of Coventry,' he announced proudly. It wasn't until that day that I realised my mother could use filthy language. She let him have it left, right and centre.

'How dare you do such a thing without talking it over with me, Eddie? You know we were supposed to go and join up with my family. You know how much it means to me that they see our new babies, and that I see them.'

'It's my life too,' he hissed. 'I've got lots of ideas. The shop is in a really a good position and I know what I can do here.'

Mummy sat down on the side of the bed, her shoulders slumped. She knew that she couldn't turn up to see her family with four children on her own because that is just not the Romany way. It's frowned upon not to stick by your man and divorce is almost unheard of in a Romany family. The full realisation of her situation struck her. She screamed at him, 'You're a control freak, Eddie. You always have been and you always will be.'

'I'm the man of this family. We will do things my way. The sooner you understand that, the better.'

Mummy had never felt so trapped in all her life.

She knew now in her heart that this was not the man she thought she'd married. Everything clicked into place like a jigsaw puzzle and she saw how he'd been dying to separate her from her family from the beginning.

Mummy's brothers had warned her, but she had wanted to believe that he was her Prince Charming. Mummy started crying, but then she turned her back on her husband and made herself stop. She was her mother's daughter, she told herself, and she would not let him see her cry. This one he had won, but from here on in, she would be one step ahead of him. She knew his game now. He didn't feel man enough, he felt inferior to the real Romany men, and this was his way of making himself feel better. There was a reason why she should have married into the race, and it was right before her, although she knew many gorger men would not behave like this. She had believed he was a good person deep down, but now she knew she could never really rely on him to put her or their children before his own silly ideas.

SEVENTEEN

Cracked China and Broken Hearts

It was sad when the fair broke up, all that cheerfulness and gaiety packed into boxes on wheels and hauled away. Most of the travellers were going to another site, a large fair at Ilkeston, near Derby. Others were going to different gaffs, or fairs, and they cheerily made plans to meet their fellow travellers when they left. But we were going nowhere. We were staying in Coventry.

We drove back into the centre of the city, in all its desolation. It was a far cry from the small market towns of Lincolnshire, surrounded by the undulating fens. Or the village of Ingoldmells, where the smell of the sea was carried on the breeze and the excitements of Skegness were there for us every day. Now the dusty city, with its grey buildings, greeted us as we pulled onto the site alongside the other caravan dwellers, who were all gorgers. This meant there would probably be no chance for me to make friends and I screwed up my face as I stared at Nathan and realised that my annoying little brother was going to be my only playmate.

After many explosive days of arguing and then of not talking at all, Mummy had reluctantly agreed to go and view the premises Daddy had bought. Why not? She knew that she had no choice but to go eventually anyway.

It was a shop built on a large plot of land, in which were sold household ornaments: silver tea services, chandeliers, brass boxes, plaques and the like. This wasn't what Daddy had planned for the shop, though. He had a huge sale and got rid of the goods for a price people couldn't refuse. He had big ideas and he now turned the back of the shop into a film laboratory for developing and printing, and put a team of photographers on the streets of Coventry, with Happy Snaps as their logo.

He also put a stall at the front of the shop for fruit and vegetables. As for the land at the side, he rented it to spivs (wheeler dealers) and market workers.

Somehow Daddy had managed to get permission to do all of this and had hired people to work on every part of the business, so he didn't have to man anything himself. He'd buy large consignments of a product to get the best possible price, then advertise it as being free to old-age pensioners or anyone spending £1.50 or more. It got him some good publicity – the *Coventry Evening Telegraph* carried pictures of the queue of OAPs waiting to be served their freebies!

He told Mummy he didn't expect her to get involved in his businesses – she had the children to look after. She wasn't able to do readings and earn a living because Coventry wasn't a holiday destination, so she was effectively isolated and dependent on him. He would leave early in the morning and arrive home very late at night. Sometimes he'd stay away all night, claiming he'd been to Evesham, which was known for its market gardening, and where he said he could get better prices than at the Coventry wholesalers. Sometimes he went to Birmingham. In her heart, Mummy knew these were not business trips.

But despite how unhappy we all were in our new circumstances, Mummy was determined to make the best of the situation. One morning, a lorryload of nursery soil was delivered, along with a vanload of plants. My mother, much to the amazement of everyone on the bombsite, set to and built a garden around the bus and the vardo. She wanted to make it feel more like a home for us, as she herself felt like a fish out of water here. There were around two dozen wagons scattered on the site, a few belonging to gorger people who weren't travellers but just wanted somewhere to live.

One couple who were parked quite near us, were called Mr and Mrs Ben. She had been in a horrific accident and her face looked as though it had melted. Her eyes were like currants in a bun. One would have thought she would be a depressed person, but she was chirpy and comical and had a very handsome husband who worshipped her. They seemed to be so happy and they had two little children. Even now I still admire the spirit of Mrs Ben and the love that this family so obviously shared.

Two doors down was a coalman, Mr Clark, who had a very dirty-looking wife. She had long, black, greasy hair which hung down her back. Her podgy face was covered in blackheads and she stank of stale pee. She had a little girl of about three years old who apparently never saw the light of day or got any fresh air. We were told that she never went out to play and was never taken for walks. We would see her poor little face pressed to the windowpane every day, looking desperate for any sort of interaction with the outside world.

Being such a large woman, no one knew that Mrs Clark was expecting again, so the whole community was surprised when Mr Clark announced they had a new baby girl. About three weeks later, my mother, returning from shopping, walked past the caravan and heard a baby screaming alarmingly. She ran back to our vardo, dumped her shopping, went back to the Clarks' wagon and began banging loudly on the door. When there was no answer, she went inside and a few seconds later fell out of the door, spewing and coughing, her eyes watering. She took a few deep breaths and then flew back into the caravan, and what she described afterwards was disgusting.

The baby had fallen off the filthy bed onto the floor. The entire floor, Mummy said, was covered in faeces. Piles of it everywhere. The three-year-old was, as usual, looking out of the window, as white as milk and, like the baby that was screaming, as naked as the day she was born. Mrs Clark was asleep on the bed, hugging a gin bottle. My mother picked up the baby and placed her next to her mother, where it at least looked cleaner than the floor. Mummy came straight out and called the authorities and later we watched them go into the vardo, fully expecting them to bring the children out and put them into care. By now, the other occupants of the vardos and some gorgers from nearby houses were standing around with folded arms in huddles, gossiping and waiting to see what was going to happen. We were told to stay indoors. Mummy closed the door, but we peeped through the windows, watching the proceedings. The authorities left the wagon without the children, much to our astonishment. It was unbelievable.

When Mr Clark came home, he spent three days scrubbing and cleaning the caravan. He had apparently been told that if he didn't keep it clean, the children would be taken to a home.

A week later, the baby died. We watched a tiny white coffin being delivered to the caravan and, to our utter horror, it was carried out and placed on a coal lorry. The family climbed into the cab and drove off to the cemetery. The memory of that little white coffin being loaded onto the coal lorry has stayed with me all my life.

On the few occasions when Daddy *was* home, more and more rows erupted and Mummy started to feel happier when he was away, as she knew her children wouldn't have to witness the tension between them, which had become all too obvious.

Although my father had many gorger friends that he had met through work and, since arriving in Coventry, in the pub who he would wine and dine with, my mother did not. Daddy liked it this way and it was almost like he was living a double life. Because Mummy had never mixed with gorgers, she was beginning to feel more and more isolated without her family and other travelling people around her. Things got a bit better when a couple of families we'd met at Hearsall Common pulled up onto the site. They'd decided to settle down, send their children to school and open some hot dog stands locally. I was over the moon, as now I had three girls my own age to play with, and Mummy was glad to have other women she could talk to.

Still, she didn't want her children growing up in the gorger way and Daddy used this as another way of keeping her completely reliant on him. She was beginning to feel like a prisoner. She was even more horrified when she received several visits from the school board, who were trying to insist that Nathan and I went to school. Daddy was fined several times for not complying.

She also knew it was only a matter of time before her husband overreached himself financially. He always did. History had repeated itself far too many times, and the part where he spent more than he was earning to impress those around him was coming again. He had already bought an American Studebaker car and half a dozen bespoke suits from the best tailors around. Who was he trying to impress? Mummy knew it wasn't her.

I'm sure outsiders would laugh and comment on the fact that, as someone who gave readings, she should have foreseen that it wouldn't work, but when you are so close to something, it's hard to see the obvious for yourself. From the outside looking in, we see things so much clearer. And besides, where our own lives are concerned, we all want to believe in the fairy tale, don't we?

Daddy never spent any time with us children, and if he did it was only to tease us or show off some fancy new gadget or car he had bought. As I gradually became more and more aware that he wasn't what a father should be, Mummy could see in my eyes that I'd been let down by him.

Mummy could never forget the day, years before, when she had cooked fish for the family. Money had been tight back then, but she had managed to find enough cash to buy something nutritious for her children. As she served up the mackerel and went back to the kitchen, she heard my father say to me, 'Don't eat the brown bit of the fish, child. It will poison you, don't you know?' I was just a child at the time and didn't know any better than to believe everything my father told me. My stomach turned and even though I tried to pick at the lighter bits of the fish, I was worried about what they also might do to me and soon pushed the plate away.

Within minutes, Daddy had picked up my plate and was eating as much of the fish as he could stuff into his mouth, brown bits and all! What kind of a man takes the food from his child's plate when they're hungry? My father's kind, unfortunately.

Mummy knew my father's businesses would go

under eventually; they all did sooner or later. That, she hoped, would be her chance to be the main bread-winner again and to get us back to her family and the safety of the Romany way of life.

With everything that was going on between my parents, I remember feeling at this time that I had become a nanny to Nathan and the twins. Worse, I felt as if I was getting the blame for everything; whatever I did, I would somehow finish up being in trouble for it. I remember, when preparing for a journey, packing some of my mother's Crown Derby china. I wrapped each piece individually in thick newspaper, but when we arrived at our destination, several of the best pieces were broken. That kind of thing is one of the hazards of travelling, but even though my mother was very good about it, I was terribly upset. I tried to make amends when she and my father were out by getting hold of some glue to stick the pieces back together again. It was a fiddly job and, while concentrating all my attention on the china I was fixing, I forgot about the pot of glue, which got knocked over and spilled its contents on the carpet.

I tried to mop it up with a damp tea towel, but that made it set even more quickly, so I tried a dry tea towel. That didn't work either, so I put the tea towels in a tub with some soap powder to try to boil the glue out of them, and I got on my hands and knees to scrape the carpet clean. Just as I seemed to be making a little progress, the pot boiled over and there were suds everywhere, spilling down the cooker and onto the carpet and, incidentally, on me. Feeling like I was in a Laurel and Hardy film, I turned down the gas to let the pot simmer and then went back to cleaning the carpet. Before long, a funny smell had me sniffing, just as I heard my parents returning. The tea towels had boiled dry.

They were horrified at the scene before them. And the china was still broken. They could hardly have been greeted by a more miserable scene if I'd been playing some kind of a practical joke. The tea towels and the pot I was boiling them in were burned and blackened. A film of sudsy glue covered the cooker, and the carpet, saturated with soapy water, had a hole in the middle where, in my determination, I had scraped right through. Needless to say, I was never put in charge of packing the china again.

Although it's funny in retrospect, I think I was reaching that awkward stage in life when I had begun to feel more and more of an outsider as it really seemed that no one understood me.

EIGHTEEN

A Fowl Idea

'Hurry up, Eva, for God's sake!' My father was drumming his fingers impatiently on the table.

'Give the girl time to eat her breakfast,' Mummy said. 'And don't wake up the twins!'

I hurriedly finished my toast and tea and then rushed around, brushing my hair and trying to find my shoes. Leaving the nice warm vardo at 6 a.m. and getting into a cold car was not something I looked forward to of a morning. But, at ten years old, it had become my daily routine.

My father had told me that I would have to go to work with him, as he needed extra help, so I learned how to do developing and printing for his Happy Snaps business. Photos had to be ready within one hour, so I was kept really busy with the many photographers he employed. And when there was not much business for the photographs, I was busily employed sorting out the bad fruit from the many boxes of produce that were sold at the front of the shop.

As Christmas was coming up, he'd had yet another brilliant idea. He went and bought long balloons, which he showed me how to blow up and twist to make little dogs. To bring them to life, I would paint on eyes, a nose and a mouth with radium shoe dye, using a little paintbrush. I would then tie them to a stick and they were sold from the fruit stall to the passing trade. They were quite a novelty, but I had to make them all on my own and, believe me, after blowing up dozens of these I would find myself feeling more than a little woozy.

Mummy objected to the fact that I was away all day when she needed help with the twins and Nathan so, much to my relief, I was eventually allowed to stay at home. It was still hard work helping to look after the other children, but at least it was work I was used to. In those days there were no such things as disposable nappies; we used terry towelling ones with a muslin lining which were fastened at the front with a large safety pin. These all had to be washed in a dolly tub, which was a corrugated bin in the shape of a barrel. Soap flakes and hot water were added to the nappies (after they'd been emptied, of course!) and we would use a dolly peg, which was like a cow's udder on a stand with handles, which we would place in the water and twist so as to move the laundry around in a manner similar to that of a washing machine. I found it much easier to sing while I was doing this, so that it was done with a rhythm.

Just up the road from where we were was a big Co-op where I would be sent to do the shopping. All regular shoppers were given a serial number, so they got their dividends, and to this day I remember our number – 637003. For £5, I would come back with about six bags of shopping. I would take the twins' pram, as I was too little to carry everything on my own, and I would ferry the shopping home in it.

One day, Mummy and I were out shopping with the pram and decided to call into my father's shop as we needed some fruit and vegetables. As we went in, Daddy was standing very close to a quite attractive young woman, their heads together as they talked. He saw us and immediately came forward.

'Laura!' he said heartily. 'And Eva! My two favourite girls. What can I get you?'

Even as a child, I picked up on the fact that he seemed flustered and anxious for us to go. As he hurriedly shoved carrots and potatoes into a bag, the woman left the shop and Daddy immediately seemed to relax.

It happened a few times after that. We'd call in and there'd be another woman present, chatting and

laughing with my father. You didn't have to be clairvoyant to realise he wanted us both out of the way. I
was too young to fully understand what was going on
but, of course, Mummy did. I think by now she didn't
really care.

Then, one midsummer's day in 1950, my father
returned from work and announced that we would be
moving. Both Mummy and I could have jumped for
joy, immediately thinking that we would be going to
join the rest of the family. Unfortunately, this wasn't
to be the case.

'We're going to Bedworth,' he announced.

It turned out that in Bedworth, a mining town about
five miles from Coventry, was a field owned by a Mr
Malcolm. He allowed fairground families to stay there
and many would pull in during the winter, so they could
repaint their stalls and caravans. People who had rides
would have to erect them to repaint them, and so it
made sense to open up at weekends. And although they
didn't take a lot of money, it was better than nothing.

Although going to Bedworth was not what we would
have picked if we'd been given a choice, it couldn't be
any worse than where we were. As we pulled in, I
remember groaning when I saw the tap where the
travelling people would get their water, as I knew I
would be the one who would have to lug our two
chromium-plated water cans up the hill every day.

There were only two other families staying, it being the summer – an old blind lady, the widow of a showman, who would sit outside her caravan all day, and another widow with a couple of children who could no longer travel. They welcomed us warmly and we soon felt at home, certainly more at home than we had in the middle of Coventry. Both my mother and I hated not having anything other than housework and child-care to do. She longed to give readings again and I longed to hear the stories unravel.

The Malcolm family, whose house was at the mouth of the field, had two girls roughly the same age as me: Yvonne and Gloria. Yvonne and I hit it off. She had a tendency to boss people around – and I liked that in her! I was so happy to meet them, thinking I'd have friends at last, but unfortunately the sisters attended a convent boarding school, so they weren't around as often as I would have liked.

To my delight, I found there was a library not far from the stopping ground. Travellers didn't qualify for library tickets because they had no permanent address, but since these were the only places I could get books, I had started to join libraries wherever we were by using false addresses. Every time, I was scared they'd know I was lying but they never seemed to figure it out. So I was never short of books, which I always returned before we moved on to another place, another library. But Mr Malcolm had said that I could use his home address, so, together with my mother, I went in and joined legitimately for the first time. The librarians knew Mr Malcolm and his daughters and were very friendly. I couldn't believe it; never before had it been so easy or straightforward to join a library.

This time, I decided to see if there was anything written about the Romany people. I was quite upset and disappointed that the books I did find were terribly inaccurate. I remember one illustrated book in which the women were pictured wearing low-cut blouses, showing their bosoms, which in our family would never have been allowed, and most of the older women were shown smoking pipes. The way we were portrayed couldn't have been further from the truth. It was then that I decided I would one day write my own book, to set the record straight.

If they were remotely approachable, I'd try to make friends of the librarians, and that repaid me on more than one occasion. We would sometimes leave Bedworth for a short trips and would park up in a country lane. Usually within hours of our arriving there'd be a banging on the door and we'd find a policeman standing there.

'I'm sorry, you can't stay here,' he'd always say. 'The limit is twenty-four hours, in case of an emergency, and that's it. You'll have to move on tomorrow.'

I was haunting the local library at the time and confided in the librarian. She kindly looked up the local by-laws and told me that so long as we moved on by the length of the caravan we were within the law to stay. We quoted this at numerous policemen over the years and although I'm not sure the by-laws would have been the same in different parts of the country, no one ever checked!

As well as visiting Bedworth library, Nathan and I would spend many an afternoon watching cowboy films at the nearby cinema. The cinema's emergency exit backed onto the field and two other travelling girls and I would dance up and down the steps of the emergency exit, practising our tap routines; when there was a musical being shown, we would pretend that the music was our very own orchestra.

One day Mummy said, 'Eva, go to the shop and get me some steel wool.'

'Why does she always get to go to the shop? Why can't I go?' Nathan immediately whined.

So my mother turned to him, put her hand in her purse and gave him the money. 'Go on then, Nathan. Get me some steel wool, boy.'

As soon as he was out of the door, I was on my feet and looked at Mummy mischievously. 'You can follow him,' she winked, 'but don't let him see you.' Nathan was, after all, only nine years old.

I dodged in and out of the wagons and cars so that he wouldn't see me. Although he did glance over his shoulder two or three times, once he'd satisfied himself that he wasn't being followed he broke into a run, as did I. Once through the field, the high street, with lots of shops, was to the left.

I saw Nathan shoot into the wool shop and shoot out again and I hid myself in the doorway of the bakery until I saw him run past. Again, I followed him and slipped into the vardo just behind him, in time to hear him saying, 'They haven't got any, Mummy.'

Mummy and I killed ourselves laughing when I told her he'd been to the wool shop to get steel wool! He didn't realise that steel wool was for cleaning pans and was to be found in a grocery store. Poor old Nathan's face was a picture. That was the last time he asked to go to the shops for a while.

Although the people of Bedworth were used to travellers, we did cause much consternation one night. The twins were in bed and Nathan and I were sitting in the vardo when Mummy got up, tied her new silk headscarf round her head and went outside to fill the kettle from the chromium water tank. Suddenly, a gust of wind blew it away.

'My scarf!' she shouted. I jumped up and went to help look for her new piece of finery, but it was too dark and even though the scarf was brightly coloured, it proved impossible to see where it had gone.

'I'll go to the vardo and get a torch,' she announced. A few minutes later, she came back out. 'I can't find one,' she said, 'but I've got an idea.'

She rolled up two of my comics (I loved the *Dandy*, *Beano* and *Eagle*) into batons and then lit them from the campfire. We ran around, searching and screeching to each other: 'Look over here' and 'You check by the hedges' and 'Leste dikes the cuver?' ('Have you found it?').

After twenty minutes, the scarf was found and we were both in stitches at how crazy a search it had been.

The next night my father went to the local public house and returned earlier than we'd thought he would. 'What's wrong, Eddie?' my mother said. 'Did you miss me?'

'Not that, Laura,' he said. 'I wanted to make sure you hadn't all been burned at the stake.'

'What on earth do you mean?' she laughed, with a quizzical look on her face. 'They stopped doing that to our kind a long time ago, didn't you hear?'

'Well, they may begin again if you keep on carrying on like you did last night. I've just come from a whole pub of people talking about us. The word is that a load of witches were seen last night doing a dance and chanting in the dark, waving lighted torches around. They wanted to know who they were putting a spell on.'

My mother started laughing. Who would have thought that a silk scarf could produce so much trouble and scandal?

One night my father arrived back from the pub and announced that he was now the proud owner of a chicken farm, won that evening in a hand of poker.

'What the hell do you intend to do with that, Eddie?' my mother snapped.

'I'm going to sell it, you silly woman.' Things were always so easy in my father's world as he never thought about the practicalities of anything.

'Who's going to feed the chickens and collect the eggs and clean them?' my mother yelled, knowing it would be any of us but him.

My father turned round and looked at me, and my heart sank. So, at the age of ten, I became a chicken farmer.

I would go to the local store to buy the chicken feed and a brown powder that you mixed with it and that I later learned was to make the eggs brown. Then I'd walk to the nearby field where the chickens were kept. I used to see the chickens pluck the worms from the ground and swallow them and, when I collected the eggs, I would think of the little worms inside them. I have never knowingly touched eggs or chicken since that time, or anything else that flies.

After a couple of weeks, I was attacked by a cockerel, which pecked my leg, making it bleed. I hobbled home, shaking, and after she'd patched me up, my mother said to my father, 'That's it, feed your rotten chickens yourself or get someone else to. She's not going over there anymore.'

My father got rid of the farm pretty quickly after that.

From then on, when my mother used to make cakes and Yorkshire puddings, she'd wink and me and whisper, 'It's OK, I've made it without any eggs, but don't tell the others.' The liar!

As the summer slipped to autumn, the field started to fill up with vardos. Soon it became a sight for sore eyes, with the show people bustling about, proper show wagons – not gorger ones – and built-up rides and stalls. I always looked forward to the weekends, when the fairground opened. The music and atmosphere becomes a part of you and there is no other feeling or experience like it. To watch people's faces and expressions when they were flung backwards and forwards on the twister or when they won a prize on the hoopla was better than going to the movies – and I'm sure I learned many words and saw many sights that would have been given an X rating at any cinema. I certainly learned a lot about life from watching all the young people canoodling right outside my bedroom window!

Mummy would put her boards out on the weekends and would do a little business, but not many people came to the fair, so she was never busy.

As one year slipped into the next, this pattern was repeated. The travellers came and went, but we had to stay. Summer was almost desolate, as our friends were away making their living, bringing the excitements of the fair to towns around the country. Then, gradually, their wagons and lorries would chug into the stopping ground for the winter months and life and colour would return.

I'd find the time in between my chores to go out and play with the other travelling children. There was one particular game we loved to play. All our lighting and cooking was by Calor gas and the empty tanks were great for walking on. We would all start in a row and see who could walk the furthest on top of them before falling off.

Our radios were run with accumulators which had to be taken to the hardware shop to be charged up – we had four, and two would be charging up while we used the other two. Every other day we children had to go and exchange the accumulators. But we found something far more fun to do with them. On the top of the accumulators was a kind of black tar-like substance and we used to pick this off and chew it instead of chewing gum – it didn't particularly taste of anything, as far as I can recall. It was from here on in that I became a tomboy, chewing my black tar and playing cricket and football with the boys.

I would rather do this than sit around with the girls, who would talk about make-up and boys; this didn't interest me in the least yet. My only girly passion was knitting, and I would often knit the twins cardigans and sweaters in the evenings, once it had got dark outside.

NINETEEN

A Tragic Accident

As was the usual pattern, the longer we were at Bedworth, the less we began to see of my father. He would leave for work early in the morning, then come home to us for his tea most evenings, have a wash and a shave, put on a clean shirt and go over to the local pub. We were used to it and didn't miss him. Mummy would ask me to watch the children some evenings while she went to the phone box to call her family – they would call each other at pre-arranged times so they could stay in touch. It filled the time a bit, but also reminded her of the life she had lost.

We did manage one trip to Whaplode, in 1953, to see the family. Although Granny was in her sixties by now, she had never been to the cinema. I was desperate to go and she was finally persuaded to come with Mummy and me one evening – it felt like we were all on a date as we got dressed up. We asked one of my uncles to give us a lift to Spalding, and Granny settled down between us in the cinema. We chose to watch *Knights of the Round Table*, and Granny stared at the screen in awe as the story unfolded. In one scene, a horse was injured in a fight and fell to the ground, where it lay dead.

'Isn't that horse a good actor,' I whispered to Mummy.

'Don't be silly, child,' Granny laughed. 'That's not a real horse; it's only a film.'

She was very wise, but also very innocent.

One day while we were in Bedworth, I was on my way back from the shops when I noticed a beautiful antique desk on the ground near our caravan. It was made of dark oak that still smelled faintly of beeswax polish. The front folded down to make the writing ledge, and there were lots of little drawers at the back that fascinated me.

It was standing on the ground next to Siddy Roper's lorry. The Roper family had settled almost next door to us, as they had daughters of my age and our parents thought we would be good company for each other. Siddy was a fairground traveller with several stalls. A giant of a man, tall with broad shoulders, he was extremely strong. Most nights he'd knock on our vardo's door to go to the pub with my father. On his way home, full of beer, he would bend a lamppost almost to the ground, and on his way to the pub the following day he would bend it back up! This was a source of great amusement to the travelling people.

Siddy knew I loved to read so he waved at me and called me over, telling me to have a rummage through the books he'd picked up alongside the desk – he must have been to a house clearance, I think. But at first I was more interested in pulling open those little drawers, all of which were empty. Or so I thought. I was fiddling around with the desk when a secret drawer came out, full of letters.

'You can't read those,' Siddy said. 'They're probably love letters. Give them to me. But if you want any of these books, just take them. They're no good to us – none of us can read.'

Mummy picked up a book called *Come and Be Killed*. 'I'm going to read it one day,' she said, and indeed she kept it for years. She never did learn to read it though.

One book seemed to speak to me, so I picked it up. It was a biography of a pianist called Eileen Joyce who was very popular, as popular as Vera Lynn at that time. I was about fourteen and it was the first grown-up book I'd ever read. It was hard, but her life gripped my imagination. She was born in a tent in a mining town in Tasmania, to a Spanish mother and Irish father. As a teenager, about my age, she moved to Leipzig to study the piano, and then went to London. She was very beautiful, but tragically her husband was killed in the war. Reading that made me cry. Whenever I had any time to myself, I'd curl up and lose myself in her story.

That book was a turning point for me. From then on, it felt as if my reading improved by leaps and bounds. By now the twins were about five and I started trying to teach them to read. Nathan was too proud to ask me or accept help but, much as I had done, he went about learning on his own.

My newly acquired skill with words became known eventually and I was frequently asked to write letters for other Romanies. Before long, I knew the typical Romany letter off by heart. It went like this: 'Dear [whoever it was], I hope you are well, as this leaves us all well at present. Mummy and Daddy send love to yours. Hope So and so and So and so are keeping well [this could be a long list of So and sos]. How are the children? We are at [wherever they were going] next week. Where are you?'

My spelling was still awful and I used to write 'dear' as 'der', but the letter would be read at the other end by someone semi-literate, like myself, so I suppose it made no difference. Even today, I receive letters that are virtually identical and give practically no news at all. All the important news is saved up until the next time we all get together to have a good old crease.

Having always wanted to be able to read and write, now that I could, I felt as though new doors had opened in my life and I could do anything I put my mind to.

I started to take an interest in astrology at this time. A gorger woman called Mary, who was married to a fairground worker, had studied it and was only too happy to give me the benefit of her knowledge. In return, Mummy would give her ten shillings now and then, as well as advice about her problems. I loved those sessions with Mary and couldn't get enough. Astrology isn't something you can learn quickly, but I was becoming quite cunning at finding people who were interested in it. The female librarian was my ally, telling me who had taken out books on the subject – if I knew them, I'd ask them about it. I also used to hang around that section of the library for hours, watching for someone to take out an astrology book. I managed to befriend one or two.

I tried to put what I was learning into practice, watching people to assess their characters, and therefore their star signs. I'd then ask them their date of birth to see if I was right.

One night there was a loud banging on the door of the vardo. My father was busy putting on a smart suit and tie, as he'd been invited by a travelling family to go to a wedding reception at a nearby hotel. The son of a man he knew was getting married; I think the family were carpet hawkers. Mummy opened up, revealing a smartly dressed Siddy Roper on the steps.

'Evening, Laura. Hey, Eddie,' called Siddy, 'I'm coming with you.'

'I can't bring someone who hasn't been invited,' my father protested.

'Ah, they won't mind. What's one more person at a big bash like that?'

'Siddy, I can't take you,' Daddy said.

Ten minutes later, as Siddy cheerfully persisted, Daddy realised he couldn't actually stop him from tagging along and gave up.

It wasn't so long ago that Siddy had received some very bad news: his father had died. He was distraught and didn't know what to do, so he started running, right out of Bedworth and into the country. He just kept on running until he came to some cows in a field. He wanted to get rid of his frustration and anger, so he went into the field and started punching one of the cows. He told my parents that he couldn't stop and carried on until the poor beast fell to the grass dead. He felt terrible remorse afterwards and every time he had a few drinks he would go on about it until people were fed up with hearing the same story. That was Siddy. A well-meaning man, but with a confused violence inside him.

As the two men were heading out of the door, my mother caught my father's arm and held him back.

'Don't go to the reception,' she whispered urgently. 'You know Siddy will drink to much and say or do the wrong thing. Take him to the pub instead.'

'It'll be all right,' Daddy said.

He was back two hours later, shaking as he told us what had happened. At the reception, the bridegroom had accidently knocked Siddy's drink out of his hand and Siddy immediately punched the poor boy, who fell backwards, hitting his head on the brass footrest around the bottom of the bar.

The fall killed him stone dead.

Afraid that the family would take immediate revenge, my father and another travelling man grabbed Siddy and ran him to the nearest door, hoping to get him out of the way before the groom's family realised what had happened. They hid Siddy in the back of the other man's van, covered him with some tarpaulin and told him not to move.

'I told you he'd be trouble, but this is bloody unbelievable,' my mother said, aghast.

'That's all very well, but what do I do?' Daddy interrupted.

'Your only option is to get him to go to the police and let them deal with it,' Mummy answered. 'They'll probably lock him up and throw the key away, but at least he will be safe in their hands. I blame you! If you hadn't taken him, all would be well.'

The next morning my father and the owner of the van drove to Coventry, making sure they weren't followed, and put Siddy on a train to Birmingham. They gave him some money and told him to stay with some of his family. They agreed he would phone the pub each night and they'd keep him posted on what was happening. Mummy and Mrs Roper went a couple of evenings, so that Mrs Roper could speak to her husband. She was a very quiet woman and I think she needed my mother's support.

Eventually, Siddy sent his brother over to fetch his family, after the bride and groom's families had gone. But it didn't end there. The story we were told was that although Siddy was reunited with his wife and children, every time they looked out of the vardo window, one of the poor dead boy's family would be standing there. They never approached Siddy, but he was followed everywere and at night there would be knocking at the windows, although whoever it was remained in the shadows. He knew people were waiting for him and he went to pieces. We heard he ended up in an asylum, where he died.

Not long after Siddy killed the bridegroom, my father's businesses in Coventry went downhill because by now he was allowing too many other people to handle his money. My mother and I agreed that it was probably due to his neglect, as he was having such a good time out and about that he wasn't taking care of business. He still hadn't learned his lesson, and by now Mummy was sure he often had other things – or other women, I should say – on his mind.

TWENTY

My Brother the Hero

'Why should we stay here being miserable? You go off all day, God knows where. You're in the pub all night. It's no life for me and the children,' Mummy told my father.

I was outside the vardo, so didn't hear his mumbled reply. I did hear Mummy shout, 'You won't go to Skegness? Well, I'm not staying here, and now you've lost your precious shop, you've no excuse. I'm giving you two choices: Skegness or Rhyl in the morning!'

We'd been in Bedworth for four years, and for my mother that had been a long, miserable time. God gives us all a gift, whether we are singers or clairvoyants, and he expects us to use it. But for most of the year she had no chance to use her gift. Moreover, before she married she'd been her own person, earning her own money doing what she loved. She hated the fact that now she had to ask my father for money to buy food and clothes.

215

Some travellers who had recently arrived at the fair told us that they had just come from the seaside town of Rhyl in North Wales. My mother quickly asked, 'Have they got palmists in Rhyl?'

'No,' they replied. 'We didn't see any.'

Knowing that my father would never take us back to our people, she decided Rhyl would be the next best thing.

Sure enough, the day after she laid down the law to my father, we packed up and hit the road. By now we'd sold the bus and vardo and replaced them with a much bigger vardo with room for us all. My mother made herself comfortable in the car and said, 'Before we go to Rhyl, we're going to the Epsom races.'

Daddy pulled the car to the side of the road, turned the engine off and got out. He stomped round to the passenger window, leaned through and said, 'Now, do we carry on to Rhyl or Epsom? Just let me know, I'm only the driver.'

As he puffed away on a cigarette, I realised my mother had the upper hand and my father was nervous, and something clicked in my mind. She had caught him out with another woman. I'd had suspicions for a while now, but the pieces had only just fallen into place. When I was older, she confirmed this was true, and it wasn't the first time.

'I fancy a flutter,' Mummy said. 'Let's go.'

Me with my cousins Honour, on the left, and Daisy, on the right. They were two of my closest friends growing up.

Nathan, on the left, with George Newsome. They met at the stopping ground in Seaton Carew and went on to become life-long friends.

Me manning the candy floss stall at the amusement park in Seaton Carew, while my father made money snapping away on the Aptus camera.

With Margaret Newsome, George's
sister, who I made friends with as
soon as we arrived in Seaton Carew.
This picture was taken just after
I had traded in my dark locks for
a peroxide blonde French plait.

Nathan posing in front of the Grand H
in Brighton. Mummy could sense we w
have a bright future there.

Me with my friend Eileen at the Regent
Ballroom in Brighton, where dances were
held every Saturday night. I loved to dance
all evening and really let my hair down,
but Nathan was always close by to make
sure I didn't dance with any boys!

The photos taken of me and Mummy by the lovely little old lady who used to stop me in the street. I had no idea that she was a famous royal photographer.

My mother used the nam
'Madam Eva' as her wor.
name, while the family alv
called her Laura. It was.
long before people noticed
two new palmistry booth.
Brighton and business
began to flourish.

As well as running my f
ever palmistry place, I wc
also work at specific ever
such as big parties or cha
evenings, which was hov.
began to build my reputa

Giving a reading to actress Phyllis Calvert at the charity ball held by the Evening Argus at Brighton's Regent Ballroom, 1962. That was my first taste of what it was like to hobnob with celebrities!

Strolling along Brighton Pier in 1962. All of a sudden my career seemed to be taking off and I was loving my new-found freedom and independence.

Writing my columns for the Evening Argus on my very first typewriter.

My Johnnie – the first and only ma[n]
I ever loved. He wasn't a Romany,
and my fear of disappointing
my mother and of losing my
independence led me to keep turnin[g]
down his offers of marriage. But
I wasn't sure how much longer he
could take my rejections.

While Johnnie was away, I threw myself into my career, which was getting better and better all the time. Here I am giving readings to Michael Crawford, Bob Monkhouse and Vera Lynn.

*Even the prospect of reading th[e]
Beatles' hands couldn't keep m[e]
away from my Johnnie! Whe[n I]
thought I might have lost him [for]
ever, I realised I could never li[ve]
without him, so at last I was
ready to say 'yes'. Our weddi[ng]
day was the happiest day
of my life.*

We made good progress that day and went to bed with the radio on, as usual. The next day we were up and ready to go at 6.30 a.m. As we drove, my mother pointed out the different trees and we passed a large field of lavender, a beautiful hazy purple, the heavenly smell drifting into the car. I was eager to arrive, as I'd never been to a racecourse before.

Unbeknown to any of us, my mother had arranged to meet up with some travellers she knew, and they had fixed for her to open up for palm-readings. She took us off to find them, leaving my father to set up the vardo for business. I hardly remember what the adults said when they got together – I was too busy keeping an eye on the twins, who were running around, while also taking in the atmosphere and the crowds. Bookies were shouting the odds, waving their arms, and little groups were huddled together checking the form and sharing their knowledge of the runners. The whole place was buzzing with excitement and anticipation.

Eventually, Mummy shepherded us together and took us back to the vardo. Once inside, she said to my father with a worried look on her face, 'Big Sam is here, and his cousins'. I'd heard my mother speak of them before. Big Sam was big trouble wherever he went. He and his pals went around in a gang and were known to have stolen lead from church roofs and even mugged people. Travellers sharing a stopping ground with him knew not to leave anything valuable outside their wagons day or night, as it would walk.

A voice came over the tannoy announcing that the first race was due to start. Mummy called to my father, 'I want you to place these twenty-five pounds on Never Say Die to win.'

'That's too much, Laura,' Daddy said, and tried to talk her out of it, but she was adamant. He went off shaking his head. The horse was being ridden by eighteen-year-old Lester Piggott, who had never won at this course before.

Mummy, Nathan and I listened to the race, hearts beating. We shouted out as the commentator announced that Never Say Die was the winner! 'I knew it!' shouted Mummy. 'Six hundred and twenty-five pounds and my stake back!'

That was a large sum in 1954. My father turned up two hours later, pale-faced, head down. 'You never put the bet on, did you?' Mummy said. He shook his head apologetically. I felt like punching him, but Mummy sat in silence for a moment, then just said, 'Bring my next client, Eva.'

That evening, when all the races had finished, my father took our two chromium-plated water cans and headed off to find a tap to fill them. When he returned an hour later, his face was bloodied but he was holding onto the cans for dear life. He told us Big Sam had tried to buy them from him, but he knew he couldn't sell them – they were a wedding present and very precious to my mother. Big Sam had then tried to take them by force. Luckily for my father, some men standing nearby had intervened and taken my father off to the hospitality tent, out of harm's way. They'd bought him a large whisky to steady his nerves after his ordeal. If it wasn't for the whisky inside him, my mother would have made him drive off the course there and then.

The journey to Rhyl was magical. The countryside was green and lush, with open fields of mustard, like yellow carpets, then fields of green crops and newly ploughed brown earth ready for planting. We saw lambs jumping in fields (and would open the windows and shout, 'Mint sauce!') and drove through lovely little villages. I wondered who lived in the pretty cottages, and tried to see into shop windows and decipher pub signs. We passed old stone churches, which I'd read were built in straight lines across the country, and I wondered how this could be possible. I tried to imagine the old fences and gates being built around fields. My favourites were the old farmhouses, surrounded by barns and outhouses. Every scene was new, and everything fired my imagination.

My happy mood would only be broken from time

to time by my father announcing, 'We're low on petrol, keep your eyes open for a garage.'

When we arrived in Rhyl, we found the amusement park, which was owned by Mr Twigdon, who was from a very famous fairground family. We found the whole family to be very nice. Mrs Twigdon and my mother hit it off immediately. They had two sons who helped to run the park, John and Clive. The twins were now six, Nathan was twelve and I was fifteen.

My mother opened her palmistry booth and my father took a hoopla stall and a darts stall. Mr Twigdon gave Nathan the job of driving a miniature tram for children, which had a track that went all the way round the park. It was his first job and he was damned good at it. Even then, he could take a car engine to bits and put it back again. It was a piece of cake for him.

My jobs were looking after the twins, keeping the vardo clean and shopping and cooking, so we had plenty to keep us all busy. Both my mother and I, though, agreed that Rhyl wasn't our kind of place, as lovely as it was. I longed for her to have what I knew she wanted so desperately, and that was to be back with our Romany family, living the life we loved.

Each day I would take the twins along the seafront, where there was a Follies show. It was always exactly the same show day after day, but it kept the twins quiet. They'd laugh and clap at the same moments every day and eventually they would shout out some of the lines before the actors could – much to the annoyance of the audience. Anne and Eddie were very good together, playing games and keeping each other occupied, but this did sometimes lead to mischief.

My father had a bag full of pennies and halfpennies which he used for change on the stall he ran. One day he complained that the bag was getting lighter and he asked my mother and I if we had taken any. All of a sudden, I realised what had happened and immediately ran next door to the penny arcade. Sure enough, there stood Eddie and Anne, feeding the penny slots with our pennies! My father moved the bag and kept a closer eye on it after that.

We didn't really have to worry about them at the amusement park, as all the travelling people kept an eye on each other's kids; only when it was really busy did we have to ground them. Eddie loved to fiddle with things like broken clocks, which he could take to pieces and then put back together again. Anne was a dolly girl; I used to knit little dolls for her to play with.

One morning, when packing the beds away, I found a dirty, wet dwile (cloth) that we used for washing the mud from outside the vardo and cleaning the floor wrapped around one of Anne's dolls. She had obviously been using the dwile as a blanket for her doll, so I decided to make her some nicer ones. I embroidered flowers on them and they looked very pretty, yet Anne still preferred the dwile!

Nathan would do his share of babysitting, and when it wasn't very busy he would put the twins on the tram that he drove around the park, on the seat behind him. They would love this for an hour or so, but when they were fed up, they would shout for me. When they were discontented, I would take them into the vardo and we would make cakes; they would be allowed to put the jam on the tarts or the cream in the sponge. They loved jelly – so much so that they wouldn't let it set, but would attack it with soup spoons, slurping it up.

I arrived home about four o'clock one day, in time to get the tea ready, to find everyone singing Nathan's praises. Apparently, as he was driving the tram, which was full of young children, towards the powerhouse, he saw lots of smoke coming out of it. The powerhouse supplied all the electricity for the rides and shows in the amusement park, including the tram. Nathan put the brakes on and ran to the powerhouse door. Despite all the smoke and fumes, he managed to turn everything off. Suddenly all the music died, as did all the rides. He backed out of the powerhouse, rubbing his eyes, which were full of smoke, to be faced by Mr Twigdon and several other men.

When Mr Twigdon saw him, he shouted, 'What the

hell have you been doing?', thinking that Nathan had caused the chaos. But once Nathan had explained what had happened, everyone realised he'd saved the day and he became a local hero.

Meanwhile, the Twigdon boys were having great fun teasing me. John Twigdon, who was twenty-two, upset me more than anything. John was a very large fellow and used to find it amusing to wolf-whistle at me when he saw me. I was tall and very skinny and was embarrassed about my figure. John had a dog called Major and, one day, Major decided to chase after me. 'Come back, Major,' called out John. 'It's not a bone!'

I was horrified and would go out of my way to avoid John and Major. This certainly didn't do my confidence any good, as I was already more than a little self-conscious.

Mr Twigdon not only ran an amusement park, but also owned a garage built alongside it. He knocked on our vardo door one day and asked me if I could spare an hour or two to work at the garage.

'Your dad said to ask you,' he went on. 'My lad hasn't turned up today and I'm stuck.'

'Give me ten minutes,' I replied. With that, I took the twins to my father's stall and lifted them over the front.

'OK, they're all yours,' I said briskly.

'Hang on a minute . . .' he started.

'But you've told Mr Twigdon I'd help him,' I pointed out and strode off. That will teach him, I thought.

My two hours at the garage turned into two weeks, from ten until four, and then I'd pick up the twins from my father and take them back to the vardo to feed them, and it was back to the usual routine.

One evening a week I'd go to the cinema with Rose, a travelling girl two years older than me. I didn't really have any other friends there, so was happy to go with her. She'd drag to me to a café for coffee after the film – but it wasn't coffee she wanted. Rose was hunting for a man and would always start up conversations with boys. I didn't approve, and one night I told her so. That ended my weekly trip to the flicks!

So the season drew on and, as autumn came, it began to slow down. My mother decided that she and I could take half a day off and go to the market, where she bought new outfits for the twins, all the incidentals and food. As we were leaving the market, she spotted a stall that was selling coats. Mummy fancied a red mac that was hanging there and she asked how much it was.

'It's four quid, love,' said the stallholder.

My mother looked in her bag and said to the man, 'Can you keep it for me until next Saturday? I seem to have run out of money; I've only got ten shillings left.'

With that, it started to rain and the man on the stall laughed and said, 'You need it now, love!'

Mummy laughed with him and asked if she could take the coat and come back the next week with the rest of the money. Surprisingly, the man readily agreed. She asked him for a receipt for the ten shillings and also told him where we were staying.

The following Saturday it was peeing down. We agreed that we couldn't possibly go out in that weather and that we'd go to the market the following week. However, on the following Thursday, a police car pulled up. Two gavengros (policemen) got out of the car. After speaking to Mummy very briefly, they put her in their car, but not before they'd told her it was about the red mac. She quickly called out for my father to go and find the receipt and told him where it was before she was driven off in the car.

Daddy went into the caravan, searched it for about an hour and came out, worriedly scratching his head, saying, 'It's not there. I can't find it.'

He went down to the police station and managed to talk to my mother, telling her he couldn't find the receipt she needed for her freedom. She glared at him. 'Go and look again,' she demanded.

One of the policemen told my mother that if she signed a confession, nothing bad would happen to her. 'You'll probably just get a telling off by the judge. It won't go to court.' Not knowing about these things and wanting to get back to her family as quickly as possible, my mother readily signed a confession.

It did go to court. They must have kept her in the cells, rather than give her bail, as she didn't come back to the vardo. My father called my aunts – the family always had the number of a nearby pub or garage where everyone could be reached – and Adeline and Vera drove through the night to get to Rhyl. They wanted to get a lawyer, but my father refused and insisted that he could speak for his wife.

He couldn't find the receipt, though, and whatever he may have said did not persuade the magistrate. My mother was sentenced to two months' imprisonment in Winson Green Prison in Birmingham. It was another black mark against my father, as far as my family was concerned, and created a scandal that was talked about for years.

I was devastated for my mother and couldn't believe what was happening. I was a witness and knew the truth, but no one wanted to listen to me.

Knowing nothing could be done about it, I told my father he'd have to look after the twins, as I was going to have to open the palmistry booth to put some food on the table. A lot of people were asking for readings.

I always looked younger than my age, so in order to do something about it, I asked some of the travelling people in the park for help. One of the girls made me up and did my hair. She told me that my clothes were too young and lent me some which made me look a bit older. I was ready for work.

I was already well trained in the art of palm-reading, but there's no doubt that the experience I had during those six weeks really helped me to gain confidence in my trade. Talk about being thrown in at the deep end! I'd never done readings on my own before – previously Mummy had picked the right clients for me and always listened in. It was exciting, though, and I loved it. My father stopped a few clients after they left the booth and asked, 'Was she any good?' According to him, they all said yes. He may have just wanted to boost my confidence, but I didn't have any complaints.

If the clients got into a subject that was a bit too grown up for me, I'd say that they really needed to talk to my mother and they could have a free reading if they came back. It didn't happen too often though – in spite of the make-up, they could see I was quite young.

Mummy served six weeks of her sentence. It felt more like six years and time dragged tremendously for all of us. I can't imagine how she must have been feeling, locked up in a tiny cell, treated like a criminal. She never discussed it, apart from once telling me she'd got a job in the kitchen, so at least she never wanted for food.

Finally she was released and arrived back in a taxi, obviously furious. She marched into the caravan and went straight to the top cupboard, opened the door and pulled out the missing receipt. I felt sick with guilt on seeing that the receipt had been there all along and I hadn't looked for it myself, just trusted that my father would have found it if it had been there.

She placed it in my father's hand, but the only words she said were: 'Tomorrow you take me and my children to my family in Whaplode.'

She snatched the receipt out of his hand and walked back to the taxi, shouting to me, 'Av akai with mandi' ('Come with me').

'Look after the twins,' she barked at my father.

We drove straight to the police station and told the cab to wait for us. We marched in there and it shook me when I heard my mother say, 'The bastard who intimidated me into signing a confession, I want to see him now.'

He came out from a back room and she shoved the receipt in his face. 'See what you did?' she said. 'See what you did?' The silly man was trying to apologise. 'You're six weeks too late,' snapped my mother. 'Just be sure of your facts before you do this to anyone else.'

I was never so proud of her as I was at that moment.

With that, we jumped back into the cab and went home. She gave the driver a very nice tip, I remember.

Back in the vardo, she did not look at or speak to my father. She just dressed the twins in their best, told Nathan and me to get changed and said, 'Come with me.' She took us to a lovely restaurant where we had a meal and all the ice cream the twins could eat and we stayed there until very, very late.

When we arrived back that night, she told me to tell my father to be ready to drive us home to Lincolnshire the very next morning.

Without saying a word, my father did indeed drive us the next morning, but not in the direction my mother had instructed. Before we knew it, we were heading not towards Lincolnshire, but to Seaton Carew in County Durham.

TWENTY-ONE

Teddy Boys and Teddy Bears

My mother and I were not happy. No one was speaking. My mother wouldn't talk to my father and he was too scared to talk to her. She told me that if she could drive, she would have driven us to Lincolnshire herself. He complained that she was like a firework waiting to explode, and he was right. How he had the audacity to drive her to Seaton Carew instead of home, I'll never know. The only thing I can think is that he was too afraid of what her family would do to him.

As for my mother, she felt deeply ashamed that she did not have control over her life. She knew that my father would indeed have got the beating of a lifetime if he'd taken us back to Lincolnshire, but as far as she was concerned a few bruises on him would be worth it for the happiness and stability our family would get from being back among our kind. Instead, here we were in Seaton Carew, next to the town of Hartlepool. It had Victorian houses and hotels, built in its heyday, golden sandy beaches and a promenade with beach huts lined along it.

It also had Collins' Amusement Park, owned by a well-known travelling family. Most of the men in the family were called Pat or John. It had been like this for generations, and it was no different for the current Mr John Collins. He'd taken over the park a few years earlier, and had added a figure of eight roller coaster and a Ferris wheel, amongst other attractions.

Across the road from the amusement park was a hotel and a lot of travelling people were staying on its grounds – as were we. So we only had to walk across the road to get to work. Once again, my mother was given a palmistry booth.

Although I hadn't wanted to go to Seaton Carew, when I realised there was a Romany family on the stopping ground and lots of travelling families with girls my own age, I felt like I was in heaven!

The season hadn't yet started, which gave us time to get the palmistry place fitted out, and my father also bought a candy floss stall and a rollertina. This is a round stall that has ten miniature horses with riders on them. Each person playing the game has a wheel in front of them and the number of their horse, and when a button is pressed they have to start winding the wheel around. The first person past the winning post hears a bell and knows they've won.

I quickly made friends with the other travellers. There was Margaret Newsome, who was my age, and her brother George, who was Nathan's age, so we were well palled up from the beginning. We hadn't been there very long before the Langton family arrived. June was also my age and there was another boy of Nathan's age, Ronnie.

Nathan didn't meet Ronnie in the best circumstances, though. The day Ronnie arrived, Nathan went to the tap in the yard to fill up our water can. As he walked towards it, he spotted Ronnie doing the same thing and both boys began to speed up, to see who could get to the tap first. They both arrived at the same time and began fighting to get control of the tap. Before we knew it, they were punching each other and rolling around wrestling on the muddy ground.

Ronnie's father spotted them and grabbed them both by the scruffs of their necks, dragging them back to his caravan. 'Don't you dare move,' he growled at them. He went into his caravan and returned with two pairs of boxing gloves, which he threw at them. 'If you want to fight, at least do it properly.'

That was the first of many boxing matches that Ronnie and Nathan had, and it was also the beginning of a firm friendship.

One evening the Collins family had a party in their wagon – a birthday party, I think. Mrs Collins came in with a tray of homemade iced lollipops. 'Gin lollies, dear,' she said to me conspiratorially. We all tucked in enthusiastically. It only took one lolly to convince me I was drunk. I was giggling and up for anything. So when one of the boys caught sight of the figure of eight roller coaster close by and suggested we should see who could climb the highest, I not only agreed but declared I'd go first!

Clutching a bottle of nail polish belonging to Mrs Collins, I climbed my way up the wooden and metal struts. When my arms and legs were aching so much I couldn't go on, I painted my initial as proof of where I'd got to. Beat that, I thought smugly and, ready to descend, I glanced down.

Oh my God, I was high! Below me, the amusement park stretched away to the sands and the partygoers cheering me on looked tiny. I froze with fear. My arms were wrapped round a strut, clinging on for dear life.

'Come down, Eva,' they were shouting.

'I can't!'

When they realised I wasn't moving, they went for help. Some showmen with ladders had to rescue me. When I tried to explain to my unhappy parents what had happened, blaming it on Mrs Collins' alcoholic lolly, Mummy said witheringly, 'Gin doesn't freeze.'

I had been high on no more than adrenalin! At least I didn't have a hangover the next day.

I got into trouble another time for taking action against a very annoying couple in a stall near to ours. As a favour, I used to boil the kettle for them (as we had an electricity supply) and make them tea. It started to feel as if they were constantly badgering me and they almost always asked when I had a big queue waiting for candy floss.

'Another cup of tea, dear?' they chorused one day, for what felt like the tenth time.

'Can't you see I've got six people waiting?' I snapped. As I made their tea, I felt very put upon. Nathan was there, and I knew he had a supply of stink bombs. I took one and, walking past their stall, I let it off. The smell was disgusting, and the crowd in front of their stall immediately dispersed, gagging and holding their noses. I hadn't covered my tracks very well and they were furious. Of course, they complained to my parents and I was grounded for a week.

I grew out of my tomboy stage eventually and Margaret, June and I became virtually inseparable. We all liked the same film stars and Pat Boone, who sang 'Love Letters in the Sand'. We also loved Elvis Presley, whose record 'Teddy Bear' was being played everywhere.

One day we heard that two older travelling girls from the park were going to take a bus into Hartlepool to visit the local dance hall for an evening of live music and dancing. I had never been to a dance hall and neither had Margaret or June, so we were desperate to go along.

When she heard that some of the older travelling boys were going to chaperone us, my mother agreed to let me go. She took me out and bought me the most beautiful gold and honey-coloured taffeta dress, held in at the waist by a gold belt, as well as some gold sandals with a small heel. I knew there was no way I would be able to jive all night in my new shoes, but I didn't care as they made me feel more grown up and elegant than I'd ever felt before. I was sixteen and my embarrassingly skinny figure was now becoming something of an asset rather than a setback. I was so excited. The day after my mother had come out of prison, she had taken me to buy my first bra. Now she was stuffing it full of cotton wool for me!

We had a wonderful time and danced so much that I was aching all over by the time we left! On the way home, one of June's brothers, Anthony, was making overtures to a gorger girl from Seaton Carew and he said to her, not knowing any better, 'I think you're class with a capital K.' The whole bus started laughing. Spelling was never my strong point, but even I knew that one! We had all had so much fun that evening that a trip to the dance hall became a regular Saturday night out.

A few days later we learned of a place called Joff's, which was a dance studio above an orange warehouse. The smell was wonderful! Here you could learn all the latest jive steps. The ambience was like an adrenalin shot and it was always too soon to leave. One boy at Joff's was brilliant at jiving, so much so that every time we went we'd say, 'I hope the boy in the white shirt is there.' I'm not sure we ever found out his name, but he did come wandering through the park one day, and Margaret grabbed him and pulled him over to me at my father's candy floss stand. I was so excited to see him, I took him to see Mummy.

'This is the boy from Joff's, Mummy, the one who can really jive!'

Mummy looked him up and down as he stood there self-consciously. 'Go away!' she said. He rushed off as quickly as he could while I stood there mortified. I now realise that she was worried I was interested in him, but there was no chance of that – he was a fantastic dancer but a bit of an ugly bugger!

The last thing she wanted was for me to be showing interest in a gorger boy. By now, the local boys were dressing like Teddy Boys. They would strut through the park with their duck's arse haircuts, so called as that's exactly what it looked like they had on their heads. They would mostly wear black drainpipe trousers, jackets of various colours that hung below the knee, and bootlace ties. And their shoes were something else, with rubber soles about an inch or two thick which made them bounce when they walked. They were full of confidence and all the gorger girls used to go crazy for them. But as they walked past we would hum the theme tune from *The Munsters*, to imply they were walking like Herman Munster!

In the evenings, after the park had closed down, all the travellers would go to the park's coffee bar, where we would sit and talk and laugh about the things that had happened, the sights we'd seen. Having friends outside of my family and spending the evening doing the things I chose to do gave me my first real taste of independence and made me feel I was living my own life for the very first time.

The Saturday after we had first gone to the dance hall, we found ourselves back there again, filled with just as much excitement. Seven or eight of us were sitting in a booth shaped like a horseshoe, with a table in the middle. We were good girls, sitting there drinking our Coca-Colas. We weren't going to do anything to risk our parents stopping us from attending these dances and didn't need alcohol to fuel our excitement and fun.

Suddenly I heard one of the girls say, 'Oh my God.' Our heads snapped up and we all turned to look in the direction she was looking in. Walking across the room was one of the most handsome guys we had ever seen off the screen. He had the build and features of Rock Hudson, with jet-black hair, and was wearing a black suit, white shirt and a dicky bow, something you didn't see at the dances. We all drew a deep breath and then continued talking excitedly.

We were deep in conversation when, all of a sudden, I became aware of someone standing in front of me and I looked up to see it was the Rock Hudson looka-like. He smiled politely at the girls before turning to me and saying, 'Will you have this dance with me?' I immediately looked at the other girls, who were looking back at me with a mixture of excitement and envy. We never danced with gorger boys, but this one was worth breaking the rule for. As I stood up, I gave my girl-friends a naughty wink. We danced two or three slow dances but didn't speak, and then I sat back down. He seemed to disappear and I didn't mind. I felt great that he had chosen me out of our group, but thought that was the end of it.

Then, just before the last dance, he came and stood in front of me again. 'What are you doing tomorrow night?' he asked.

'I'm babysitting,' I quickly replied.

One of the other girls looked at him and said, 'Tomorrow night from seven thirty we'll all be in Toni's Coffee Bar in Seaton.' He thanked her, said goodnight to us and left.

The next night, the girls all arrived at my caravan and said, 'Come on, we're going to the coffee bar. Quick, Eva!' They were going to make sure that I turned up. Reluctantly, I agreed to go with them. I knew the other girls went on dates, but it wasn't something I'd ever done or felt comfortable with.

As we approached the coffee bar, I stopped. I must have had a feeling. I said to the girls, 'Go and look through the window and see if he's there.' Two of them casually sauntered past the window, then turned round and walked back again discreetly. They came and stood at my side with wide eyes and said, 'Oh, Eva, go and have a look.'

I had to see what they looked so wide-eyed about, so I walked over to the window. There he was in all his finery: a green Teddy Boy jacket, complete with bootlace tie. I went back to the group laughing. 'I'm going home, girls, he's all yours.' I was relieved, to be honest.

The summer was now drawing to a close and we decided to stay in Seaton Carew for Christmas rather than go away and come back again next season. By this point we had all made friends there, including my mother, who had become close to Ivy, June and Ronnie's mother, and Bella, who was Margaret and George's mum.

The Christmas of 1955 holds some odd memories for me and is definitely one I shall never forget! We had been in Nottingham a few months earlier for the Goose Fair, and while we were there Mummy decided she was so fed up with watching me struggling with my hair, she would take me to what she had heard was the best salon in town. So we duly arrived at what looked like a very expensive hair salon, in the centre of Nottingham. Mummy asked the receptionist, 'Who is your very top stylist?'

A very dapper man glided into the salon and lisped, 'I'm Mr Christian.' After fingering my hair for a while, Mr Christian asked, 'How would you like it styled?'

My mother said, 'You seem to know what you're about. Do what you like. I leave it entirely to you. Just make my daughter happy.' And with that, she gave me a peck on the cheek and left us to it.

As it was my first experience in a salon, every time he asked me something, I didn't know what to say and just nodded nervously. I was excited and desperate to see what he would come up with for me.

Within three hours, the dark hair had gone and a peroxide blonde emerged, with a French plait. Nowadays the blonde is gone and I have returned to my dark-brown colour, but the French plait remains. Like many women of my age and era, it quickly became my trademark look.

A few months later, as Christmas was fast approaching, my father and I popped out one cold December afternoon to buy a few Christmas presents for the rest of the family. My father still had his Studebaker, a big, black, shiny monster which ate petrol but which he loved, as it was very powerful and good for towing our vardo. I think the main reason he loved it was that it was equipped with all sorts of luxuries which you just didn't get in British cars and it was, of course, flamboyant. So there I was, sitting alongside him, with my new hairstyle and hair colour, courtesy of Mr Christian.

What we didn't know when we set out was that witnesses to a £75,000 bank robbery, which took place in Nottingham that same day, had described the robbers as being a tall, good-looking man with curly hair and a moustache – my father, to a T – and a young blonde who was described as looking just like me! Added to which, they had escaped in a big, black American car.

My father had left the car in the car park, unlocked, with the logbook in the glove box, also unlocked. Obviously a spot check was being carried out on all American cars and a quick glance at the logbook showed that the Studebaker had last been taxed in Nottingham. We were visiting a few shops nearby, knowing nothing of all this, and when we returned to the car after only ten minutes or so we were suddenly surrounded by uniformed police and detectives.

An important-looking policeman with pips, a peaked cap and a triumphant look on his face yanked open the driver's door and barked at us, 'We've got you!'

'What? What are you talking about?' my father cried. 'We haven't done anything wrong!'

We were so startled by it all that we probably looked like we were guilty. The police wouldn't listen to us, but bundled us into their car and took us to the station. I couldn't help laughing as it was so ridiculous, but I was very scared too. After all, look at Mummy, who had been perfectly innocent but had still been locked up. Would that happen to me too?

Gradually, as various reports came in, the man in the peaked cap began to look less puffed out with pride and the brightness in his eyes dimmed. It took about an hour to prove that we couldn't have been the bank robbers they were after and then, without a word of apology from old PC Plod, we were allowed to go. That was a relief, but it taught me one thing: I would hate to be a thief. The whole scenario had frightened me even though I knew I was innocent – I can't imagine what it would feel like to know you were guilty. But at least it gave me a good story to tell. That will forever be the Christmas I was arrested for a bank robbery!

I cannot claim that a good relationship exists

between Romanies and the law. We never think of policemen as being our friends and seldom expect to be protected by them. That just seems to be the way things are and the way they have always been.

In olden days, if a child disappeared, it would be said that he was stolen by the gypsies, although I would have thought that Romanies had enough children of their own to worry about without going around trying to steal more! More recently, if anything was stolen and gypsies were in the area, they'd be the first to get blamed. Granny always taught her daughters to be careful when doing readings in someone's home – 'Don't allow yourself to be left alone in a room, in case something goes missing later and you are accused.' Some people say that gypsies have a persecution complex, and maybe they have, but that's because they are always being persecuted. I know that is a strong word, but it is a feeling common among us.

Discrimination against gypsies exists within the legal system. The Highways Act makes it a criminal offence for a gypsy (or a hawker or itinerant trader) to encamp on a highway. There are still many prosecutions brought against us every year under this act. No wonder we don't not consider the police our friends.

The myth of thieving gypsies is so strong, moreover, that the arrival of any group is often a signal for local criminals to get to work, knowing full well who will be the first targets of the police. Being so often wrongly blamed, we do tend to have a good deal of sympathy with those who have the law on their tails.

I remember once a man arrived at our vardo late at night and my father invited him in. They had done some deals together in the past involving motorcars, and the man spoke a few words of our language. After a few minutes of general chat, he told my father that the police were after him and he wanted somewhere to stay the night. We let him stay and, next morning, the man left early. Later in the day, the police arrived, looking for him. They were told that nobody had seen him. I must emphasise that my father knew the man quite well and was convinced that it couldn't have been anything really bad he was mixed up in or he would have turned him away. The crime in this case was being in possession of some stolen tyres, or something like that. But my father knew that, however minor the crime was, the full force of the law would be brought down on his friend regardless.

TWENTY-TWO

Coming of Age

Like a thief in the night, adulthood crept up on me. One day I woke up and I was twenty-one. I touched the wall of the vardo next to my bed. It felt the same. In fact, as I looked around, I saw nothing had changed. I felt disappointed. Life was just the same. I didn't even feel any older. I wouldn't have been so disappointed if I had known of the big party that was planned for me, though, and even less so if I had known of the events that were going to change the course of my life before I saw my twenty-second birthday.

After two years in Seaton Carew we had moved to Northampton for a few months, and then on to a field near Wilby Lido, on the outskirts of the market town of Wellingborough. And there, thanks to my father, we had become stuck again. He was now making a living selling Siemens vacuum cleaners and had a team of men who went door to door demonstrating them. My father argued that it was becoming more and more difficult for travelling people like ourselves to find stopping places of any kind and so we should stay for a while.

It was a permanent site with an electricity supply, so we were able to wire up the caravan, and there were lots of other facilities as well. It was also very conveniently situated for us, in a fairly densely populated part of the country, which meant my mother and I could go off hawking by car every day, always managing to find some place we hadn't been before. We did quite well, buying up job lots of nylon stockings, underwear and men's socks to hawk. A lot of them were seconds and were very cheap, which meant we were able to make a good profit out of them.

I'd take the twins to the pool sometimes, and we'd sit and watch people swim, but I would never go in. For one thing, I was too self-conscious about my body to bare it in a swimming suit and, more importantly, I'd been terrified of water since the day my father had thrown me in the sea. But one day, when there was no one else around, Nathan persuaded me to get into my swimming suit and lie on his lilo while he pulled me around on the water. Feeling incredibly brave, I did, and it was lovely. Until a group of boys arrived, that is. Suddenly a frog landed on the lilo next to my face. I shrieked, thrashing around trying to escape, and fell in! Nathan had to drag me spluttering out of the water. Never again, I vowed. Water and I did not mix.

On the day of my twenty-first birthday, I had a lot of presents – although one particularly special one I had to decline, at least for a while anyway. I remember Mummy bringing me in a cup of tea and slowly taking a beautiful ring from her finger and putting it onto my skinny hand. When we were in Rhyl, Mummy had a particular client who would drive down to see her once a week without fail, chauffeured by her son, Gerry, a strapping thirty-nine-year-old writer with great dress sense. Gerry wore a thick gold ring with a beautiful green stone in it on his little finger. He told us that he had found the ring in the desert in Egypt when he was just twenty-one. One day he came by our vardo and told us that he was going to live abroad. When I returned from taking the twins out for a walk, Gerry had gone and I'd missed the chance to say goodbye to him. But before I could allow myself to be sad about it, my attention was drawn to Gerry's beautiful ring, which was now on my mother's hand.

'You've got Gerry's ring on,' I said with surprise, wondering why he would have given Mummy something so precious to him. She smiled and said, 'He asked me to look after it for him.'

Now she was giving the ring to me.

'What are you doing?' I exclaimed.

'Gerry wanted you to have this ring when you were twenty-one,' Mummy replied. 'He knew he would never have any children of his own and wanted the ring to go to a good home.' Gerry and I had always got on well; for some reason, he thought I was fabulous and used to say that if he'd ever had a daughter, he imagined she would have been just like me. But I knew I couldn't take the ring, as I was petrified of losing it. I didn't feel responsible enough to look after something so special.

'But he wanted you to have it,' Mummy insisted.

I told her I would ask for it when I was ready for it, and she reluctantly agreed.

My main present from my family was to be my party, which they told me about over breakfast so I'd have the rest of the day to prepare myself. I had thought we might have a family party of some kind, so it was a lovely surprise when they told me. Most girls celebrating their most important birthday would want to know well in advance so they could plan for it. But it really didn't bother me, since there was no one for me to invite anyway, apart from the family and people living in nearby vardos, who would all come along in any case.

But when my father told me he had booked a small hall in the town, I realised it was going to be a bigger turnout than I had expected. I guessed he was using the occasion to invite along a few business acquaintances for a drink. My mother took me out that afternoon and bought me a cocktail dress which was very tight-fitting and had short sleeves and a low, square neck. It was in turquoise and inky-black silk and, though I loved it, I would never have had the nerve to choose it for myself. It was the first dress I ever wore that I regarded as a real woman's dress, rather than a girl's, and I wasn't sure, looking in the full-length mirror, that I felt like a woman yet. It seemed very sexy, the kind of dress in which one needed to be cool, confident and sophisticated, and I was certainly none of those things.

The 'small hall' turned out to be a very big club. My father was friendly with the owner and had arranged to take it over for the night. He had hired a group to play dance music for us and there was a bar and tray after tray loaded with food.

The family party had become a reception for well over a hundred people, and there were lots of fellow travellers that we had met at different fairgrounds. But a lot of the people there did turn out to be my father's business friends. I never knew he had so many! Most of them were gorgers, of course, and I had to meet them all. I was polite to them, but I felt incredibly shy. The guests I really wanted to see were my family, as they were the only ones I felt truly confident with.

At last they turned up, Aunt Vera, Uncle Cardy and their girls being first. Daisy looked absolutely beautiful in a tight-fitting brown dress and we ran into each other's arms as soon as we set eyes on each other. Her sister Honour, who looked just like Ava Gardner, arrived with my cousin Pam. Then came Cousin Johnny with his piano accordion, then my cousin Willy Taylor with his sister Vera, and then a friend of my parents I called Aunt Olga with her husband, a lovely man who looked like a gangster from films of the Prohibition era. When I saw Olga, my heart sank. She looked so magnificent that I was certain I had to look awful by comparison, especially as she was wearing the same dress as me, except hers was a more sophisticated pure black.

Aunt Lena arrived with her daughters, Vera and Lavinia, who were now making records professionally as the Hewett Sisters. My mother worked the crowd, looking marvellous in fine, black silk crepe, all ruched and figure-hugging. Having all my most favourite people together under one roof, it felt almost like old times.

Naturally, everyone had to do their party piece. Cousin Johnny took up his piano accordion and played 'K-K-K-Katy', while Aunt Vera, in a black dress with jet beads sewn all round the bottom, did a tap dance to it. Then Aunt Lena, who had the poise and husky voice of Marlene Dietrich, sang 'You Made Me Love You', which is one of our family favourites.

There was a gorger boy there called Jock Hall who

had worked for my father at odd times, and he had a really wonderful voice. He sang with the band, and Vera and Lavinia pricked up their ears immediately when they heard him start to sing. He began with 'Mack the Knife' and when he finished there was tremendous applause, led by the two girls. They went up to speak to him and, within a few minutes, they had sorted out a number for the three of them to sing. As a trio, they were fantastic, so good that no one from the outside world would ever have believed they were anything but a well-rehearsed, professional act. Jock Hall did, in fact, become professional. I got him his first engagement years later, and he went on to be a big draw at the clubs in the North and the Midlands, where he sang under the name Nat Hall.

The party was really swinging by now, but some of us were feeling a bit inhibited because of the gorgers my father had invited. We just wanted to have a real family party. So my father, after seeing my apprehension, told everyone we were finishing, but that the family would stay behind to clear up. Lots of the gorgers, who were really nice people, offered to help, but we managed to persuade them that we would be able to manage on our own, and eventually they all left.

That was when we really got going! Nathan was first, playing his guitar. We nicknamed him Tommy

Steele from then on because he bore such a striking resemblance to the star, with the same fair hair. Although I say it myself, Nathan is the most marvellous guitar player, as good as anyone I've ever heard, which is amazing considering the fact that he only ever had a few informal lessons.

One day, while sitting outside the vardo at Wilby Lido, Nathan was closely watching a man playing the guitar outside the wagon opposite. The man looked up, saw Nathan watching him and beckoned him over. 'Are you interested in the guitar?'

'Yes,' Nathan replied. 'I'm getting a new one tomorrow.'

The man offered his guitar to Nathan. 'Show me what you can do,' he said. With this, Nathan set to work and showed the man all he knew. Two hours later, Nathan came back into the vardo with a smile from ear to ear and showed us the new chords he had learned from the man. For the five days that were left of the man's holiday, he taught Nathan what he knew and the two could be heard 'jamming' into the early hours of the morning.

It turned out that the man was, in fact, Karl Denver of the Karl Denver Trio, and Nathan had been tutored by him for free from morning till night!

After Nathan played a few tunes on the guitar, somebody called out for me to tap dance, and I needed no encouragement. That went down well, or so it seemed to my slightly blurred mind, and then Nathan and I were called upon to do our speciality. This was an arrangement of 'Autumn Leaves', which we had worked out together; I sang some parts and then the guitar took over to play a couple of passages.

Each of my aunts sang something in turn before my mother played 'Around the World in Eighty Days' on the piano accordion. Then it was time for some dancing and everyone watched spellbound as my mother and father glided across the dance floor. Things may not have been great between them at home, but they always looked like they were made for each other on the dance floor.

I have no idea when the party came to an end because it was one of those fabulous evenings when time stands still. Whatever time it was, it was very late, but I remember not feeling remotely tired. Although I woke up feeling still like a child at twenty-one, at twenty-one years and one day, I woke up feeling very old indeed!

A few weeks had passed since my birthday and we were still based near Wellingborough, although the site was largely empty. I could tell that Mummy was unhappy, as once again she was unable to see clients and use her gift. But the more she went on to my father about joining her own people, the more determined he seemed to keep her away from them.

I was thoroughly on my mother's side and I found it increasingly difficult to see her looking so sad and lost. My mother was the most important person in my life and I had seen her suffer enough. I'd always been afraid to make a stand before now, but I too had had enough. I sat her down and suggested that if my father didn't want to go back to our old way of life, then we would do it without him.

I discussed it with my father too, telling him that not only was my mother unhappy, but so was I. I also told him that I was trying to force my mother to either go back to her own people with me and the other children, or make a fresh start all together, doing what we did best. I could see from my father's face that he knew I was very serious.

'But I'm doing all right,' he protested.

'Yes, and you don't get home until ten or eleven o'clock at night, while Mummy and I are sitting in a caravan in a field, looking after the twins on our own, without any of our other family around,' I cried. As long as you're all right, Jack, I thought to myself. 'Why don't you buy the *World's Fair*?' I suggested. I had never challenged my father like this before. 'Shall I go and get a copy now then?'

He nodded and I ran to the newsagent's and all the

way back, holding in my hands what I hoped would be the key to getting us out of this miserable way of life.

Lo and behold, a palmistry place was advertised in Brighton. And before the day was over, plans to go and investigate were being made. My parents drove from Northampton to Brighton and, when they returned, we started packing. No wagons were allowed in Brighton, so we'd have to sell the vardo. My mother, beaming, said, 'I found a fully furnished flat, and we can move straight into it. And guess what else,' she added. 'On the way back, your father and I stopped at a pub on the outskirts of Brighton. You'll never guess who was sat there drinking a pint each. Richard Burton and Elizabeth Taylor! The town is full of film stars!'

My father reluctantly said, 'We'd better pack then.'

Of course, it wasn't that simple. For us, moving out of our vardo and into a flat was as big a step as it would be for people about to emigrate to a country they had never seen. 'Shall we? Dare we?' were the unspoken questions in all our minds. 'No, we won't' and 'Yes, we will' were the hopelessly confused answers, varying in shades of passion according to our moods. Sometimes not a word needed to be spoken. We had only to look at each other and read each other's secret thoughts – pretty obvious, during this period – and we would burst out laughing. It was crazy. We were all like kids about to take on a dare.

As the time for moving grew nearer, the butterflies increased until they were swarming. Our feelings of excitement and fear were intense.

As with most things, the anticipation was perhaps more exciting than the actual move. I suspect that for Romanies, even more so than others, it is always better to travel than to arrive.

The tension continued to mount until the last day. In the vardo, after we had all gone to bed, we would lie in the dark thinking about what the future would be like. The silence was heavy and usually, after ten or fifteen minutes, someone would have to break it. I remember Nathan calling out at the top of his voice, 'I'm going to be a gorger!' My own thoughts ran more along the lines of: Thank God there will be no more carrying water! How luxurious it would be to have a bath and then pull out a plug, as I'd seen them do in the pictures! And no more long treks to the toilet! The pluses were beginning to mount up.

TWENTY-THREE

A Brand New Start

As we drove into Brighton, I fell in love with it immediately. We passed the clock tower and continued along the seafront, taking in the sights of all the big hotels and the Regency architecture. We turned into Cannon Place to see a charming little row of Regency cottages. As I stepped out of the car, I remember thinking, Am I having a dream? Am I actually going to live here?

Eddie and Anne were running up and down the road, whooping and hollering with excitement. Nathan and my father were unloading all our goods and chattels, which had been packed into the car. We spent a couple of hours exploring the flat and deciding who would sleep where, then we started to get hungry, so Mummy sent Nathan off to buy fish and chips for four.

'I'm hungry too, Mummy,' I said.

She shushed me and winked. When Mummy winked there was always something naughty or exciting about to happen. She looked at me mischievously and said,

'Come with me.' I followed her through the front door and she said, 'You're quite grown up now and we need to celebrate. You've never had a glass of Champagne, but you're going to have one now, and so am I.'

She was obviously very excited. We walked into the Grand Hotel, which was on Brighton's seafront, with glorious views out to sea. We made our way to the bar and sank into two luxurious seats. 'We're celebrating the move, you and I.' Her eyes gleamed as she beckoned the waiter over to us and ordered two glasses of Champagne and an assortment of sandwiches. As we waited, we drank in the ambience of this lovely hotel. We didn't need to speak. We had arrived where our dreams had led us. When the drinks arrived, she clinked her glass on mine and said, 'This is what you should have had on your birthday, to celebrate, and that's just what we're doing now. Cheers!'

'Cheers!' I beamed.

We talked excitedly about the palmistry booth, but then I brought up the fact that there was only enough room for one of us to give readings at a time. I suppose the Champagne helped me to pluck up the courage to say, 'I suppose I could find another place?' She looked a little startled and didn't say anything for a minute. Then she smiled and said, 'If that's what you want to do. I worked on my own when I was your age. We'll have a look round tomorrow.'

When we got back to the flat, we told the family what we planned to do. We then spent the rest of the night giving the kitchen and bathroom a good scrub. Not that they weren't already clean, but when you've cleaned something yourself, you know there aren't a stranger's germs around.

That was the very first night I ever went to bed in a house! What I realised, as I lay there, was that I couldn't hear the elements: the rain, the wind. It was strangely quiet, so I turned up the radio and had to turn it off again when Anne, whom I was sharing a room with, complained, 'Daddy said we've got to go to school.' She was worried and needed someone to talk to. I spent a long time explaining how lucky she was and how I would have given anything to have had the opportunity.

'But I don't want to go to school,' moaned Anne.

'But, Anne, you need to,' I urged. I decided to give up and turn the radio back on again. I was flogging a dead horse, trying to talk her into it when she had watched the rest of us live our lives with each other instead of being sent off with a load of strangers. It wasn't our decision anymore anyway. We were becoming part of a society where schooling was not an option but a legal requirement.

That night I slept like a baby, but when I woke up I had no idea where I was! It felt very strange when I realised I was in a flat and not our vardo, like every other morning of my life so far.

We settled in quite well, I suppose, considering that as a family we had always lived in one room, the same room we travelled in. Now there was no more walking miles to find a phone box, because the telephone was at hand. No more filling up the water tanks, running out of Calor gas, finding an obliging person near the site who would allow us to plug in our electric leads. From now on, with a big kitchen, we were going to be able to buy a whole week's worth of shopping in one hit. We could make the beds and not have to put away the blankets before breakfast. It was going to be a new life.

It felt strange for quite some time and even though we all loved our new home, we found ways to make sure we were all in the same room together as much as possible. Whenever I wanted to make up my face or do my hair, rather than stay in my bedroom, I would take my cosmetics or my hairbrush wherever my family were. It would take a long while for us to get used to having so much space.

There was no such thing as a two-way conversation in my family; everyone always joined in. If my mother was working in the kitchen, we would all follow her in there to tell her and each other our thoughts on a particular subject. Or my father might be shaving and whatever conversation we were having at the time would just shift into the bathroom, with everyone having their say.

Things became easier for Mummy and me once the twins went to school. Eddie was just as nervous as Anne, for in our family only Daddy knew what they could expect. It must have been very hard for them – they were twelve years old and couldn't read or write. It was obviously ridiculous to put them in with the infants, though this would have been the correct standard for them, so they were put into classes with children of their own age who had been attending school for about seven years. There was a kind of streaming system at the school – with A, B and C classes and so on – and, of course, they were put into the C class. It was actually rather amusing because, on that first day, we all anxiously waited for them to come home, hoping they wouldn't feel too inferior, and Eddie reported to us with a shrug that the kids in his class were all so thick most of them couldn't read or write either!

Funnily enough, neither of them seemed to learn too much at the school, but it did have the effect, I suppose, of giving them the impetus to learn to read and write. Before very long they both started to teach themselves and got on quite well. Anne decided that nothing was going to stop her from being able to read fairy stories to her children when she married.

It was now April 1960 and we wanted to get to work quickly and make the most of the summer season. I found a house almost opposite the West Pier that was owned by a Jewish lady who also owned a shop in which she sold fur coats. Her name was Mrs Gold.

When I approached her, she was quite agreeable about allowing me to open a palmistry place on the forecourt of her house – for a price, of course. Within three days, I had put up a garden hut up, which I carpeted inside, and the outside was adorned with a sign reading: 'Eva Petulengro. Palmist and Clairvoyant'. I furnished it with a card table covered with a beautiful silk paisley shawl, two comfortable chairs and a table lamp. I was in business!

Other travelling people in Brighton soon noticed the two new palmistry places and, as they do, came to talk to us to see if we knew any of their families. This gave me the perfect opportunity to quickly make new friends, one of whom was Iris Taylor. She lived in a big house that belonged to her parents and she was left in Brighton to look after the house while they travelled. She rented out the spare rooms and ran a hoopla stall in the arcade where my mother's place was. Iris had no travelling mates and, like me, she didn't really know how to mix with non-travellers, so we had both found a friend to go to the cinema and shopping with. It was Iris who introduced me to the local dance hall, the Regent.

Nathan was very happy to escort Iris and me around and act as our minder when he wasn't working his own darts stall on the pier. His job, Mummy said, was to look after me, which I always considered a cheek as I was three years older than he was! But I never minded, as I loved spending time with Nathan. He was also a bloody good dancer, so was hardly an embarrassment to be seen with in the dance hall. Nathan and I loved our new-found freedom. It was all so exciting. Now that the twins were at school, it was even easier for me to let my hair down.

My new palmistry business seemed to be flourishing. One pleasant day I was sitting outside my hut when a young man sauntered towards me. He was extremely good looking and was dark enough to pass for a Romany boy. He introduced himself to me. 'Hi, my name's Michael. Michael de Costa.'

'Did you want a reading?' I enquired.

'No, I just wanted to have a chat with you,' he replied.

That took me by surprise, so my nerves made me quickly say, 'I don't have time for chats. I'm here for business.'

He smiled and said, 'I'll go away if anybody wants a reading.'

My nerves started to die down a bit and I began to feel more intrigued than embarrassed. 'Are you an actor?' I asked him. He had all the hallmarks of one and my clairvoyance kicked in and made me blurt out this question.

'Yes,' he responded, and promptly started telling me about his colourful career. I could sense this young man was going places.

I told him that if I talked to him any more I could never give him a reading, as we don't give readings for friends or family – to know too much about some-body can prove very misleading for us. Sometimes what people tell us can lead us away from following our natural senses.

I liked this boy, but only as someone I found inter-esting and could imagine myself becoming good friends with. I told him to pull up a chair, but just as we started to chat properly, I glanced up to see Iris walking to-wards me along the promenade. 'Ah, here's my friend,' I announced.

I don't know what made him think of it, but he quickly said, 'Eva, please don't tell her that I can speak English. Let's have a laugh.'

I knew I liked this boy for a reason. I'm always up

for a laugh. When Iris approached us, I said, 'Iris, can you speak Italian?'

'No,' she replied. 'Why?'

'Because this fella can't speak a word of English and we've been trying to communicate with each other.'

'Really?' she said.

I nodded. She looked at him and then said, 'He's bloody gorgeous!'

Michael sat there with an innocent smile on his face. He was a good actor! Iris and I began attempting to talk to him in pidgin English.

A client approached and I went in to read their hands, leaving Michael and Iris sat outside, all the while trying to communicate with each other, or so she thought. By the time my reading was over, they were both laughing their heads off. It wasn't long before the three of us became firm friends.

Michael went on to go to Hollywood and featured in a series called *The Zoo Gang* with stars such as John Mills and Lilli Palmer.

TWENTY-FOUR

Written in the Stars

All my mother's good feelings about Brighton were proved right, as always. It was a great summer for us and at the end of it we made the decision to stay there, to give up being travelling people, for a while at least, and become the same house- and flat-dwellers that we had always felt so separate from. Why? Hard to say, looking back. For money? It was a good season, but we'd had good seasons before. It wasn't just for money. For comfort? Yes, we were comfortable in our new home and if we were going to stay, we would make ourselves even more comfortable. At the same time, we missed the close companionship of the travelling life, but, as I've already said, doors couldn't stop us from spending practically all our time together.

Was it Brighton itself? Well, we loved the town, and we loved the bracing air. It was good for business and near to London, where we loved to go shopping. But it wasn't just this. It was a combination of all these things, plus an absolute confidence in my mother, who predicted that good things would happen for us in Brighton. We were also all aware that the Romany life we had known, the freewheeling migrant tradition which had existed for centuries, was dying now – if, indeed, it wasn't already dead – and we didn't want to die with it.

When deciding to stay, my parents had to make a further decision about the several hundred pounds we had accumulated over the season and which they had hidden in the flat. There were lots of reports of robberies in the *Brighton Evening Argus*, our local paper, and Mummy in particular felt worried about our safety with the money there as a temptation for thieves, so she came to the conclusion that she should open a bank account.

I don't know if my mother had ever been to a bank in her life. But that was the situation she found herself in, and she knew we had to start getting used to the gorger customs if we were going to live in the gorger manner. So, quite boldly, she walked into the bank she had chosen (because she liked the way they decorated their window boxes), put the bundles of notes on the counter and said that she wished to start an account.

The clerk there said that the bank would require two references. Mummy was quite startled by this request. She replied, with sincere indignation, 'It's my money I'm giving you to look after. I should be asking for references from *you*!'

We only had a short lease on the Cannon Place flat, so we moved to a flat on Royal Crescent, with Sir Laurence Olivier as a neighbour on the left and John Clements and his wife on the right. When autumn came that year, I started to notice that a man who lived in a nearby flat would jump in his car and follow me whenever I left. He would pull up alongside me and offer me a lift. Despite me always refusing him, he still persisted.

'Go away and leave me alone,' I would say, in no uncertain terms.

'I'm only being neighbourly,' he would bray back at me.

I didn't tell my father or Nathan because I didn't want them to have a confrontation with him, but I did tell my mother. She immediately went and rang on his doorbell. He opened the door and she said, 'Now, young man, I want to talk to you about my daughter.'

He started laughing louder and louder. She realised he wasn't quite right in the head and she needed to be careful with him. With wide eyes, she said, 'You're a good-looking man. I'm sure you must have many admirers, but please don't talk to my daughter again. She has a very nervous disposition, you understand.' She quickly turned on her heels and returned home.

'The man's a nutter,' she said to me. 'There's definitely something not right about him.'

It was already quite strange having someone stalking me, but if my mother was now concerned, that made me ten times more worried. After the life she had led, there wasn't much that could shock her, but I could see that she was shaken. As much as we loved living in the Crescent, my mother's feelings about this man and my trust in her judgement and my own meant that we decided to move again.

There was a big luxury flat to rent in West Street Mansions, right in the town centre and next door to my mother's dukkering place. 'Not bad going, eh?' said Mummy. 'Three moves in less than a year. It's almost like travelling again.' Whatever happened in our lives, she always kept her sense of humour, a trait which got us through anything. So we moved into this big first-floor flat and that became our home for the next few years.

During our first November in Brighton, we'd heard there was to be a big ball thrown by the *Evening Argus* newspaper at the Regent Ballroom to raise money for a children's charity. An acquaintance I had made at the paper suggested to me that I might offer my services, which I did.

I was delighted when I found out I would be rubbing shoulders with people like Gracie Fields, Vera Lynn,

William Hartnell, Flora Robson, Godfrey Winn and Alan Melville. These were people I'd only seen in films or on TV. It started off with me giving readings for the general public. The celebrities were cordoned off with a big yellow rope on the other side of the ballroom. After a while, a distinguished-looking gentleman with silver hair and spectacles came over for a reading and afterwards he told me that he was greatly impressed by my accuracy. He then introduced himself to me as Mr Gorringe, the editor of the *Evening Argus*, and he invited me to go with him behind the yellow rope. He wanted me to read some of the celebrities' hands – I had to stop myself from jumping up and down with excitement!

The first person for me to read was Zena Marshall, who went on to become the very first Bond girl. William Hartnell, who later played the first Doctor Who, invited me to sit with him and Dame Flora Robson and then invited me to dance with him, as did Norman Wisdom. In the end, I hobnobbed with most of the celebrities present, including Phyllis Calvert and Leo Glenn, and I was obviously thrilled to pieces.

Before the evening drew to a close, a writer who was working for the *Argus* at the time asked me to go to the office with him. I presumed he was too embarrassed to ask me to read his palm in front of his colleagues so I followed him. But when we got into the office, I realised the reason for the invite, as he tried to pull me towards him. Shocked, I pushed him away and beat a hasty retreat.

The next day, to my delight and amazement, there was a double-page spread in the *Argus* which was very complimentary about me and my work and made me the focus of the evening. A little later in the day, I had a phone call from the editor, Victor Gorringe, asking me to go and see him. Mummy had one of her psychic flashes and suggested I draft out a horoscope column to take along with me, which I did, just in case.

It was a bit of one-upmanship on my part. Before he'd got through telling me about his idea for me to write a daily column, I dived into my handbag, drew out what I'd written and placed it on the desk in front of him. His face was a picture of astonishment as he tried to read my scrawl. He then pressed a bell on his desk and a young lady appeared. He asked me to accompany her so that she could type up what I'd written. 'You may have to dictate it to her,' he said drily.

I took the typed copy back to him and he read it. He then formally asked me if I'd like to write a daily column. Would I? Of course I would! He pressed the bell again and the girl reappeared. He put the copy in the girl's hand and said, 'Give that to the features editor to go in tomorrow's paper.' I couldn't believe it. We agreed on three pounds a week.

The next day I waited for the paper to arrive at the newsagent's. He had given me a whole page! I did this for six months before one of the reporters at the *Argus* that I'd become friends with suggested I get my copy syndicated to the other regionals.

'How do I do that?' I asked.

'I suggest you go to the Press Association. They deal with all that stuff,' they replied.

Nathan and I trotted off to the railway station the next day and got the train to London, which was only about an hour away. We took a taxi to Fleet Street, walked into the Press Association's vast offices and were greeted sternly by a tall man in a green suit and a green peaked hat who folded his arms as he stepped in front of us. 'Can I help you?' he asked.

'I'd like to see the features editor, please,' I said with my head held high.

He smiled a mocking smile and said, 'Do you have an appointment?'

I looked him straight in the eye and said, 'No, I don't. Please would you tell him Eva Petulengro is here and that I need to see him immediately. It's quite important.'

He told me I'd have to write in for an appointment, but I stood my ground and said, 'It won't hurt you to go and ask him, will it?'

He could see I wasn't going to go away and withdrew. On his return, he asked me to follow him. I was led into the editor's office, where I was invited to sit down. Nathan stood behind me. The editor studied me carefully before he spoke. He said, 'I had to see you because nobody gets past Charlie. You must have impressed him. What can I do for you?'

I took some copies of the *Evening Argus* from my bag, laid them on his desk and said, 'I'd like you to syndicate these, please.' He studied them carefully, then after a few minutes looked me straight in the eye and said, 'Yes.'

Nathan and I left the office and could hardly speak. How could it have been so simple? We hadn't eaten that day so I asked him if he'd like to have something to eat now and he replied, 'I couldn't eat a thing. You cheeky cow, how do you get away with it, talking to people like that? You should have been thrown out on your ear.'

A few days later, I received a phone call from the writer who had come on to me at the *Argus* ball, telling me a film producer friend of his wanted to meet me. He said, 'His house is just around the corner from the office, Eva. Come with me.' I was obviously wary of him, but was also bowled over by the prospect of a film producer being interested in me and couldn't pass up the opportunity to meet with him.

He took me to a little row of old cottages, rang the

doorbell and, when there was no answer, casually said, 'Oh, he can't have arrived yet.' He put his hand in his pocket and produced a key. I realised right then what his real game was, but I wasn't afraid. We went in and he put some music on and offered me a drink.

'He must have missed his train,' the writer muttered.

With this, I belted him in the eye with the hand on which I wore a very large ring – my knuckle-duster, as I called it. At the same time lifting my leg, I kneed him right in the groin, just as my mother had always instructed me to if I ever got caught in these circumstances. I left the cottage hoping and praying that his eye would go black before he got back to the *Argus* offices. It did. Not only that, one of his front teeth was also missing.

Two years later, when I had an office in East Street, a lady came in with an appointment one day and I gave her a reading. She then proceeded to tell me that she had two other lady friends who had been to see me and she confessed that all three of them had been paid by this writer to report back to him about what I had told them. He'd said he was going to reveal me as a fraud, but she said the three of them were more than happy with their readings and had decided to tell me that he was trying to screw me – yet again!

Around the time of the knuckle-duster incident, I kept running into a lovely little old lady who would stop me for a chat and would always say, 'I'd love to photograph you.' I was always in a hurry and paid no heed. However, one day, my mother said that a royal photographer whose daughter was married to one of Winston Churchill's sons had approached her. She wanted to photograph both of us.

When we arrived at the beautiful house, in a very exclusive terrace, it was my little old lady friend who opened the door. I was speechless, for on the walls were black and white pictures of all the top film stars. She truly caught the spirit of my mother in her photograph and I couldn't believe that the little old woman who I thought was merely a keen photographer was, in fact, a professional and very renowned one.

I was renting a booth in the Aquarium, opposite the Palace Pier, when one day, while I was giving a reading to a lady, three mods burst in to grab our bags. My instincts took over and I attacked them with my crystal ball. I hit one square in the chest and he fell to the ground, wheezing. My client was by now screaming and the mod was screeching obscenities.

He started for the door, but by now I was really seeing red. I had worked hard all day for my money and here he was thinking he could just waltz in and take it. I wrapped the velvet that my crystal ball was kept in around the ball and started swinging it at him.

It was hilarious to see the look of terror on his face as he ran out yelling, 'Leave me alone, you witch!'

It was reported in the local paper and my mother made me give up that place after that, as she thought I was too vulnerable there. That's certainly not what I thought, though. In fact, I couldn't wait for him to come back for round two, now that I had learned how very useful my ball could be in ways I'd never imagined.

Strange that despite my profession of foreseeing the future, I never guessed I would become a writer. Around this time we had again been talking of leaving Brighton to go back on the road. But the responsibility of writing my regular column kept me there, and then another event, which I also hadn't anticipated, took place and made my temporary stay a permanent one. I met my Johnnie.

TWENTY-FIVE

Meeting Johnnie

'I've got a date, Eva!' Iris said. 'With a boy called Vic. We're meeting at the Sussex at eight o'clock. Please come with me, just in case he doesn't turn up. I don't want to be sat there all alone. Pleeease!'

She'd called round to the flat, almost breathless with excitement. I wasn't keen on the idea of going to a bar, even though I was then twenty-three years old, because I knew my father wouldn't approve – bars weren't considered somewhere for Romany girls to be seen. But she begged me to accompany her and I couldn't let down my friend.

'I'll come, but I'm not waiting around all night for some boy,' I said firmly.

'No, we'll just give him ten minutes and if he doesn't turn up we'll go to the dance like we planned. I promise! Thank you so much, Eva.'

I was still feeling a bit cross about it as I got ready to go out that night, putting on my moss-green sack dress, which was all the rage at the time, and applying another layer of mascara and eye-liner. I just didn't understand why so many girls seemed to be just dying for a man to come into their lives. I had had the occasional date by this point, but never felt strongly enough about anyone to get romantic over them. I often used to wonder whether there was anything wrong with me. Looking back now, I can see that my life as a Romany and my work had a great deal to do with the way I felt at the time.

As a Romany, I'd had a sheltered life, which made me shy towards any male not part of, or a friend of, the family. And my work meant that although in some ways I was totally innocent, naïve by today's standards, what I lacked in personal experience I made up for in knowledge of other people's lives and problems. This gave me a sort of built-in warning device which prevented me from getting involved with anyone. Funnily enough, because of my work, it seemed that all the conversations I had with men were based on a kind of consultant–client relationship. I don't know whether this was because of their curiosity about what I did for a living or whether I needed to gain the upper hand by playing the expert, but I usually finished up advising them about their career prospects or something like that.

Anyway, whatever my feelings towards men, I

certainly liked dancing with them, and that's why I agreed to keep Iris company until her date turned up, after which I would meet Nathan and our other new friends at the dance hall. Our social life in Brighton couldn't be restricted to mixing only with Romanies, and the occasional travellers that we admitted to our inner circle. It isn't possible to live and work in a town without meeting and becoming friendly with gorgers, which is why the move from the road to permanent dwelling places has eaten away at the traditional closed existence of Romanies. My parents realised that a lot of our restrictions had to be eased and, as a result, I was allowed to mix with gorgers. Not boys, of course, but gorger girls.

Iris and I duly sat down in the plush seating of the Sussex Hotel in East Street and ordered ourselves a Babycham. We hadn't long to wait until Vic turned up, but he must have been entertaining the same kind of doubts as poor Iris, because he brought along a friend as well.

'This is John,' Vic said, introducing us to a very good-looking man, tanned and rugged.

'Eva,' John said, smiling at me warmly and holding out his hand. The corners of his bright-blue eyes crinkled up attractively.

I took an immediate dislike to him. In fact, I felt almost panicky. Oh God, not you, I thought, and then wondered why those words had come into my head. I'd never met him before in my life. I didn't want to be on some kind of double date, but at the same time I felt I couldn't get out of it, not just because of politeness, but because, against my will, I felt drawn to this man.

He was nine years older than me – not a boy, but a man. He had a lovely smile and, I reluctantly had to admit, a droll sense of humour. Most people, on learning my profession, immediately start to ask me questions about themselves, or want me to read their hands, but John didn't ask me any questions at all of that sort, and I think it was probably this that made me begin to warm to him.

When offered a drink, I asked for a Babycham, which was my favourite at the time. John smiled and ordered a bottle of Möet et Chandon. This, to me, was terribly sophisticated, but I treated the arrival of the Champagne with nonchalance, or at least I hoped it seemed like I did.

John was a yachting man and, since the age of fourteen, he had worked on boats of all descriptions, painting them, sailing them, repairing them. Just recently, his principal occupation had been delivering sea-going yachts to their owners, mostly in the Mediterranean, and no doubt he had picked up his Champagne habits from some of his rich clients. In fact, he had obviously been a bit of a playboy himself.

I'd never been the slightest bit impressed by men, apart from being madly in love with Rock Hudson, Larry Parks (who played the part of Al Jolson in *The Jolson Story*), Gregory Peck (of course), Humphrey Bogart and Tony Curtis, who could have had me any time he wanted (not that he'd have wanted to!). But mere mortals held no fascination for me at all until the age of twenty-two, when I first set eyes on Johnnie. I couldn't understand why I went weak at the knees and my heart was pumping. I felt out of control of my emotions for the first time in my entire life.

I didn't know how to deal with this loss of control, so I told myself that I'd never see him again after that night, even though I knew deep down that I would.

The next day, Iris called at the flat to take me shopping. When we walked past the coffee bar next to our building, I saw Johnnie, bold as brass, sitting in the window with Vic. They came out and invited us to join them for coffee. Johnnie was grinning, dimples in both his cheeks.

'I can't stop, sorry, errands, going to be late,' I stammered. 'You stay, Iris, don't mind me.' And I did a runner! What is wrong with you? I asked myself. You're not usually afraid of anybody or anything.

Three days later it was the weekend and a girlfriend, Eileen, was having a twenty-first birthday party. Together with Nathan and some trusted pals, I enjoyed the party, circulating and dancing to the records. All of a sudden, the door opened and in walked Vic and Johnnie. I was very much aware of him, but deliberately kept my back firmly turned away. I pretended that I was in deep conversation with a very boring girl who was, typically, asking me all about my work.

Then the door opened again and three young men arrived. No one seemed to know who they were, but after about ten minutes I heard a giggle and a shout of 'Put me down!' I turned to see that one of the boys had picked up a girl called Mo and her legs were waving up and down. 'Put me down!' she giggled and screamed, loving it. I carried on talking until I felt myself being lifted in the air. The young man's face was right in mine. I didn't scream and I didn't struggle. Instead I grabbed his ears firmly and twisted as hard as I could. It must have hurt, because he dropped me. Before I could get up from the floor, I saw Johnnie grab the boy and sling him out of the door. He then grabbed the other two by the scruffs of their necks and pushed them out too. Someone shut the door on them all, including Johnnie.

I rushed up and said, 'Isn't someone going to help him? There're three of them!'

Vic laughed and said, 'John can handle it.'

I was worried for five minutes, until my hero walked back through the door, picked up a bottle of beer and took a long swig. We drifted towards each other, just like in the movies, sat down on the floor and talked and talked and talked. He didn't even ask for a date. I think we both knew then that fate had plans for us.

Sure enough, the following weekend, Nathan, Iris and a few pals had arranged to go to the Regent Ballroom. We usually met beforehand in Andy's Coffee Bar in Preston Street, but Iris took me to one side and said, 'I've got a date. I'm meeting a guy in the Sussex pub in East Street. I can't just stand in the pub on my own, in case he doesn't turn up. You've got to come with me.'

'I can't go in a pub,' I said, horrified. 'My parents would kill me.'

'They'll never know. Please, Eva, don't make me stand there on my own.'

Once again, I let her talk me into it. As we walked into the Sussex, lo and behold, her date was Vic, and standing by his side was a grinning Johnnie. I turned to leave, but the three of them talked me into having one drink. I suddenly realised I'd been set up. And you know what? I liked it!

We all went to the dance together. Johnnie and I danced to the slow dances and didn't need to speak: 'Mona Lisa', made famous by Nat King Cole, and 'Up on the Roof' too. I went home with my brother, but not before agreeing to a date for the next evening.

My problem now was how to shake off my shadow. In the end, I couldn't see any way round it and had to confide in Nathan, and to my surprise and relief he was over the moon as it meant he could now do his own thing. But we arranged to meet at 10 p.m. so he could take me home as usual. It suited him, and he became a co-conspirator in my romance.

Johnnie and I would talk for hours. He wanted to know everything about me and my life. He told me about his yacht deliveries. He used to deliver them all around the world and, during the summer holidays in Brighton, he would run a speedboat from the pier. He told me all about his girlfriends, of which there had been many. Some of his stories were fascinating. Once, when taking holidaymakers on a hair-raising trip, a young boy grabbed his arm and said, 'Excuse me, but a lady's just got off.' When he looked round, there was a woman in the water. Her long skirt had ballooned out and saved her from going under. He turned the boat around, dragged her, screaming, out of the sea and told her in no uncertain terms, 'If you want to commit suicide, don't do it on my boat!' She complained to the pier manager, but he had saved her life.

Our meeting place was the Sussex pub in East Street. By now we had firm friendships with the landlord and landlady, Harry and Cath, and quite a lot of the characters who were regulars there. I still hadn't told my mother about my boyfriend. I felt I should be open with her, but was afraid of hurting her or, worse, I was scared she might hate me because I was going out with a non-Romany. I couldn't bear the thought of disappointing her.

I decided I didn't need to tell her because, given time, I was bound to go off him.

TWENTY-SIX

Tears and Laughter

While I was seeing Johnnie, my career began to go from strength to strength. In 1962 I was invited to go on a programme called *What's My Line?* which was presented by Eamonn Andrews. There was also a panel, which consisted of Lady Isobel Barnett, a doctor, the presenter Barbara Kelly, Gilbert Harding (the original Mr Nasty) and Gerald Nabarro, who was a Conservative MP.

The idea was for them to guess what my occupation was. As you walk out onto the stage, there is a chalkboard and you are supposed to write your name on it. As my name is Petulengro, though, Eamonn Andrews thought that everybody might guess my Romany roots immediately, so I told him that in English it translates as 'man of horses', which in turn, of course, is Smith. So on I walked and wrote the name Eva Smith. I then had to do a mime and I had agreed with Eamonn that

I would pretend to usher an invisible person into a room, as I would do a real client for a reading, and then I took my seat next to Eamonn.

The panel are allowed to ask a question each, and Lady Barnett went first. 'Do you have anything to do with food?' she asked. This, I thought, must have been because she thought I was showing someone to a table and therefore was a waitress or restaurateur or suchlike.

Barbara Kelly, however, guessed immediately. 'Are you a clairvoyant or astrologer?'

The audience could see she was correct because the board at the top of the stage gave them the person's real job in advance, and their reaction told her she was right. Before the clapping stopped, Gerald Nabarro bellowed in a loud voice, 'If you're a clairvoyant, can you tell me if my party is going to win the next General Election?'

The audience went very quiet awaiting my response. I felt a little bit stupid at that moment, as I didn't really follow politics and, to be totally honest, had no idea who he was. So I said, 'I'm sorry, Mr Nabarro, but I don't know which party you're with.' This was an honest response, but the audience obviously thought I was very clever and comedic and erupted into gales of laughter and clapping and whistles, whereupon Eamonn Andrews added, 'Well, I think a lot of people don't know what party he's with. So I think we'll close the show on that note.'

Off stage, everybody – producers and panel – congratulated me for my wit!

It was around this time that we got the news from Spalding that Uncle Nathan was seriously ill with kidney disease. Mummy went to be with him, as did all the family. The Romanies have a custom of staying with whoever is ill when they are in hospital – even if they are there for weeks. When Mummy arrived at the hospital, the doctor told her that he wouldn't last the night.

In fact, he hung on for three days. Granny, who was in her eighties now, was persuaded to go home to rest while the sisters sat outside the ward, knowing he was near the end, waiting. What do you say in these circumstances? Nathan's wife, Bertha, opened her bag and took out a pill box which contained Parma Violets for sweetening the breath. She offered the box around. Mummy took one look and heard herself say, 'What are these – purple hearts?'

The joke released the pent-up emotions of all the sisters and suddenly they couldn't stop laughing. Just then, the doctor came into the waiting room and said, 'I'm sorry to tell you Nathan has gone.'

The laughter turned to screams and wails.

Sadly, Uncle Alger died shortly afterwards of brain

cancer. And then Uncle Walter choked to death. So poor Granny lost her three sons in quick succession. It was a terrible time for her.

It was 17 November 1962. One evening, around seven o'clock, the doorbell rang and I opened it to find my cousin Daisy standing there. I yelled, 'Mummy, it's the Herons.' I found myself looking over Daisy's shoulder, waiting for the rest of the family to appear, but instead, a young man was making his way up the stairs. Daisy nervously said, 'I'm married, Eva.' That was about all she could manage, and she looked at me and waited for a response.

Mummy pushed past me. She had heard what had been said and hugged Daisy, then put her hand out to the young man and pulled him inside the flat, exclaiming, 'Come in, come in.' She looked sternly at the young man, who we would soon find out was called Sonny Boy, and said, 'Show me your marriage lines.' This is standard in our family, marriage lines meaning marriage licence. After satisfying herself, she handed the marriage certificate back and seated them in our lounge. 'Nathan, go out and get some Champagne, we're having a party!' Nathan disappeared. As is her usual way, my mother said, 'Right, you children must be hungry. I've got some lovely steak in the fridge.'

They protested, 'Maybe we could have something in an hour or so. We stopped and had something on the way.' You could see from the way Daisy spoke that she was still finding it strange to say the word 'we', as in a married unit, and she blushed as she said it. Sonny Boy Pattison was a true Romany, but from a family we hadn't met.

As Nathan poured the Champagne, Mummy looked at Sonny Boy and said, 'I bet you've got a beautiful voice.'

Daisy broke in. 'He's got a handsome voice, Aunt Laura.'

'Right,' demanded Mummy, 'later you're going to sing to me, but right now I want to hear how you two got together.'

Daisy hesitated and then said mischievously, 'Well, Aunt Laura, we'd been casting glances at each other for some time . . .' They had arranged their marriage licence and fixed a date at Long Sutton in Lincolnshire, as Daisy and her family were staying at the old bakery site in Whaplode. Sonny Boy came down from Blackpool and they left home early in the morning and arrived at the register office, but were told that they needed two witnesses. Sonny Boy went outside, dragged two people in off the street and asked them if they would oblige. They were only too happy to. This was quite an unusual event for them and they would certainly have a story to tell their families when they got home.

We were now on our second bottle of bubbly. One of the reasons they were here was to have the Romany blessing from Mummy, and the time now seemed right.

Nathan jumped up and said excitedly, 'Right, now let's have some music.' He brought out his guitar and began to play 'Travellin' Light'. Daisy stood up and started singing with him. It was an apt song for the circumstances. Afterwards, I sang 'Autumn Leaves' with Nathan and, as Daisy and I glanced at each other, we both knew this was a night we would never forget. We were no longer children. She was married now and I saw before me the woman emerging from the girl.

Nathan, Mummy, Daisy, the twins and I, urged on by the Champagne and the occasion, all started shouting, 'Come on, Sonny Boy, it's your turn.' We didn't know then if he could sing or not, but from the confident way that Daisy was joining us in our banter, she obviously knew something we didn't.

Daisy was sitting in an armchair and Sonny Boy gazed into her face. He started to sing 'You Made Me Love You' in a velvety voice which was a cross between Nat King Cole and Dean Martin. Throughout the song, Mummy and I couldn't stop crying. It was so touching and you could see he meant every word.

We learned that, earlier in the day, Daisy had sent

a telegram to her parents which read: 'Married today, sorry this way.'

A couple of months later, Honour eloped with Eric Boswell, another handsome Romany who sang like Dean Martin. We hadn't met Eric and decided to go to Blackpool to look him over. When we arrived, we found that Sonny Boy and Daisy had bought a house, as had many of the family by that point, although their vardos were always parked behind the houses – handy in case they decided to roam a bit in the winter months. In reality, they couldn't just let go of the Romany life. Whenever we got together as a family, weather permitting, we'd light a fire in the back garden and sit around it, as if we were still in a field in Lincolnshire.

Sonny Boy sat me down and said, 'Eva, I have to tell you what I did last week.' He went on to tell me that he had taken on two new stalls now that he had a wife, and he needed someone to help him run them. Daisy suggested he put an advert in the local paper, which he did – the girl in the advertising department of the paper helped him word it. He received quite a lot of replies from people who were interested and the first one to be interviewed was a young man who was so handsome that Sonny Boy knew he would attract all the young women.

He spoke to him and he seemed very reasonable, so he decided to take him on.

'Can you start tomorrow?' Sonny Boy asked.

The young man hesitated and said, 'Yes, I can, Mr Pattison, but I need to tell you something first.' He paused and added, 'I'm gay!'

Sonny Boy, not knowing what the boy meant, replied, 'Don't worry, lad, I'm a little bit gay myself sometimes.'

Later that day, he told Daisy what had happened and at the end of his tale she burst out laughing before explaining what gay meant. Sonny Boy looked at me, waiting for my reaction – of course, I did the same.

Poor Sonny Boy was worried the young lad might have got the wrong idea and was very embarrassed the next time he met him. But, in fact, it all worked out very well and the lad carried on working for Sonny Boy for years – and he was indeed very good at drawing in the women (and some of the men).

TWENTY-SEVEN

Reading Palms and Falling in Love

As the months passed, my feelings for Johnnie didn't change. I still didn't dare tell my parents, however, and we used to meet wherever we could without a chaperone on some pretence or other. I wonder if my parents suspected something. My father did try to keep track of my friends. One evening I'd been out with Johnnie, at the flat of a friend of his, playing poker. I was happy because I'd won and left having had enough excitement. But a few of the guests there that night decided to go swimming!

My father tackled me the next day. 'I understand you were at a party last night,' he said accusingly.

'Yes, playing poker,' I admitted, heart thumping in case I'd been found out.

'And then you stripped off and went diving naked off the pier!' he shouted.

'*I* was diving naked off the pier?' I asked sarcastically. 'And did I drown? Because, thanks to you, I can't swim.' Did he not know me at all? I thought angrily as I stormed off. Not only had he instilled a fear of water in me, but he should have known that I would never get naked in public.

Once, I decided to go to London to buy a leather coat. My parents didn't mind me going alone, so long as I caught the four o'clock afternoon train back. This gave me a chance to meet Johnnie, and so I did, at the station. I hadn't been able to give him much notice and he had come straight from work. He looked a sight, with diesel-stained white plimsolls, a shrunken and holey boating jersey and a dirty white yachting cap set at a jaunty angle. I probably thought he looked lovely, even though he desperately needed a shave, but to anyone else, he must have looked a disgrace.

Anyway, we travelled up to London, first class, and it never crossed my mind that we must have looked an odd couple: John dressed like a tramp and me done up to the nines in an expensive fur coat and very high-heeled shoes. When we got to the West End, I marched into a posh shop somewhere in Bond Street, with John lagging behind a bit to gawp at something. I didn't realise I had left him behind until the saleslady's smile of greeting faded and she apologised to me. 'Excuse me a moment while I call the manager. We don't encourage *that* type in here!' I realised she was talking about poor John! I walked out with great indignation, leaving the saleswoman bewildered and Johnnie bemused, wondering why I had suddenly changed my mind about shopping there.

I now had a palmistry stand on the forecourt of a hotel near Brighton's Metropole Hotel. It was just two chairs, a card table and a crystal ball inside a garden tent, but with very nice signs. Weather permitting, I was there every day. Since we relied on holidaymakers for the bulk of our trade, we never took holidays when ordinary people did, or knew what it was like to go away for a bank holiday weekend. That was when we worked, for as many hours as it took, so long as the punters were around, and that made us different from ordinary working people. But when the weather was bad, it was good, because Johnnie couldn't run the boat and would have to take the day off, as would I.

On 22 November 1963, some friends decided to drive to London and come back around 10 p.m., so I organised my alibi with Nathan and six of us crammed ourselves into the car and away we went. We went to the Colony Club, run by the American actor and gangster George Raft. It was packed with smart Americans in cocktail dresses. I wore a black pencil skirt, five-inch heels, and a blue roll-neck sweater that came down to my hips. That was the fashion in those days, but not to go to smart clubs in! After a while, I was having a problem with a bra strap. I went into the ladies, where three American women were doing their faces. I went into a cubicle, adjusted my strap and then headed for the door. One of the women turned to me and said, 'Hey, honey, you ain't washed your hands!'

I looked back at her and replied, 'Honey, I ain't touched nothing.' I really didn't like these pretentious people, and decided to give as good as I got.

Something really important was happening that night in the States. I learned the next day that John F. Kennedy had been assassinated.

Although I knew I was falling in love, I fought against it. Each meeting I had with Johnnie, I intended to be the last. I just knew that my mother would disapprove of a gorger son-in-law, so I dared not tell her about him, for fear I wouldn't be allowed to see him again.

Johnnie and I discussed this, of course, and he was very understanding. He knew that marriage was a big commitment, he knew that the odds were that it would affect my relationship with my family, and he knew how important my family was to me. I was hopeless and I don't know why he had so much patience with me. I was like the girl in the old music-hall song, who wouldn't say yes and wouldn't say no.

This went on for the best part of three years and,

eventually, he did get fed up with all my indecision. While he spent most of the year working the speed-boats at Brighton or Worthing, he still occasionally took jobs abroad, delivering yachts. He was offered quite a few commissions like this, but usually turned them down so that he could spend time with me. Then a big chance occurred: the opportunity to deliver a luxury yacht to Majorca. This was a trip Johnnie really wanted to make and he gave me an ultimatum – either I could go with him and we could make it a honey-moon trip, or he would go without me. I still couldn't rid myself of my sense of guilt, so he went without me.

I missed him terribly while he was away and I wondered whether he would ever want to be bothered with me again after yet another refusal. Our long courtship was obviously proving a tremendous strain and I knew it was all my fault. It wasn't just that I was worried about my mother's probable reaction. An even deeper worry was my own uncertainty. How could I be positive that my feelings wouldn't change? Could this possibly be prolonged infatuation rather than love?

For me, marriage was the most important step a woman could take. In my line of work, I had seen much unhappiness caused by marriages which were incompatible or where the physical attraction had died after a few years, leaving nothing in its place. I was determined this kind of thing would never happen to me. While Johnnie wasn't there to reassure me, these thoughts tormented me.

The one thing I had to occupy my mind constructively was my profession, and I threw myself into this with a will. Perhaps because I worked so hard, my career progressed in an almost spectacular fashion for someone so young and for a writer who had never been formally taught to read or write.

The horoscope column had proved to be enormously popular and was by now being syndicated to several provincial newspapers. The horoscope magazine I had recently started was also going well. The trouble with the magazine was that whenever I thought about it, which I had to do regularly, it always made me think of Johnnie, for it was he who had encouraged me to start it.

I had been glancing through one of those magazines that make predictions and, as usual for me, was criticising everything about it. Johnnie, who I don't think was really interested, had just shrugged and said, 'If you think you can do better, why don't you start one yourself?'

'Right,' I'd replied instantly, 'I will.' The decision was a typical one, impulsive and unreasoned, since I lacked financial as well as literary training. But small details of that kind never did worry me and, having said I would do it, I was determined I would. So I went along to my friend, the editor of the *Argus*, and told him, 'I want to have my own horoscope magazine. And I want you to print it and publish it for me!'

He thought I was mad, of course, and told me so. Then he started to spell out all the details: the cost of the paper, of colour printing a cover, of typesetting and making blocks for illustrations.

I knew I was lost unless I could somehow counter a lot of arguments which I didn't even understand. Fortunately, I knew his weak spot and, in a moment of inspiration, I interrupted him. 'I know, why don't we do it for charity? It will be Christmas soon and we can bring out a special issue, with the proceeds going to any charity you like.'

He blinked at me and thought it over while I waited with anticipation. He muttered to himself and scribbled some figures on his pad. Then he muttered some more and I nodded intelligently. When I could make some sense of the technicalities, it transpired he was offering to produce a one-off Eva Petulengro magazine – 5,000 copies, so long as I guaranteed a certain amount of advertising. I agreed at once, went out and sold the advertising myself and came back with it before he had even got in his printing estimates.

The 5,000 copies we turned out sold like hot cakes

and I decided that I had been right all along. I could produce my own magazine and, more than that, I now knew how to go about publishing it myself – and that's just what I did, although that is a story on its own.

At this time, I was also gaining a reputation because of the many celebrities who were my clients. From a journalistic point of view, my profession as a clairvoyant was extremely useful, since many famous people didn't want to give interviews, but were still prepared to talk to me and answer my questions, if only because they wanted to question me in return!

My father's niece was getting married in Nottingham in October 1964, Goose Fair time, and my parents had decided that the family would go to the wedding, see some of our friends at the Goose Fair and then visit my grandmother and aunt at Whaplode. It could have been my guilty conscience, or it could have been a psychic flash, but I was convinced my parents knew I was seeing someone and thought they were being clever, getting me away from him. What they didn't know was that Johnnie wasn't even in the country and wouldn't be back in Brighton for a few weeks. I was actually happy to get away so I didn't have to be in Brighton without him.

I bought a black designer suit for the wedding, together with a big, black cartwheel hat, and I teamed them with a shocking-pink chiffon blouse with frills.

But after the wedding ceremony came the dinner, which had a 'no kids' policy. Without even being asked, I was put in charge of ten children and had to entertain them while everyone else went to the dinner. Talk about a bloody cheek! I took the little people to the cinema and filled them full of ice cream and sweets every time they complained. After the movie, I returned to the hotel, where the parents took over, much to my relief. I did join in the do after that and jived like there was no tomorrow to a band and to the Beatles, who were so popular at the time. After the wedding, we went to the Goose Fair, met up with loads of people we'd got to know at fairs over the years and ate hot mushy peas with mint sauce, which was and still is a speciality in that part of the country.

I really missed Johnnie, but also knew I had big things on with work. I had just been dancing to the Beatles, but in two days' time I was set to meet the Fab Four through the *Argus*, when they visited Brighton to play at the Hippodrome. At least that would keep me occupied, I hoped.

TWENTY-EIGHT

Wedding Daze

'The Duke of Connaught, as fast as you can,' I demanded breathlessly to the taxi driver. I'm sure he must have thought I was having a heart attack from seeing one of the Beatles. Little did he know why I was really in such a state. And now, as I sat in the back of the taxi, I looked down at my grandmother Alice's gold bracelet and wondered what she would have made of what I was doing. Somehow, as I twisted the gold charms around my wrist, I knew that she would have done exactly the same thing, and I smiled. I smiled and then I started laughing and suddenly I couldn't stop. The tears were literally running down my cheeks and so was my mascara and, do you know what? I couldn't have cared less.

When I spoke to Johnnie on the phone, he said, 'Are you going to marry me? How quickly can you say yes?'

'Yes!' I shouted.

When my taxi drew up outside the Duke of Connaught pub, Johnnie was standing outside waiting for me and rushed to open the door. He looked tanned, but his handsome face was spoiled by a beard and moustache.

'Lose the beard,' I said, not very romantically, before throwing myself into his arms.

Inside, a bottle of Champagne was waiting for us on the bar, compliments of my good friends Eddie and Pearl, who happened to be there. We sat and enjoyed the Champagne and decided to get a marriage licence the very next day. The time flew by and too soon I had to get back in a taxi and head home to West Street.

I was in a bit of a state, wondering if my mother would guess what was happening. Nathan, bless him, was sitting on the stairs waiting for me. He grinned and said, 'Can't let you go in on your own, gal.' He grabbed my arm and we went in to find a party of sorts was taking place. My uncle Laurence had unexpectedly arrived that evening for a visit. Most Romany visits aren't planned; they just happen. Uncle Laurence had been married to Aunt Cissie. Poor Aunty Cissie had been diagnosed with a bone-crumbling disease shortly after giving birth to her only daughter and had to spend the rest of her life in a wheelchair.

I was given yet another glass of Champagne, which

helped dull my nerves and trepidation tremendously. Everyone crowded round me and Nathan, asking about the Beatles. The conversation seemed to go on for hours before Mummy declared that it was bedtime. Daddy and Laurence were to share my bedroom, and I was to go in with Mummy. I lay awake most of that night, worrying whether I should tell her I was getting married. If I did, would my parents stop me? Would they put me in the car and drive away? The anguish was terrible – I so much wanted to tell her, but I was too afraid.

The next day, Johnnie and I went to arrange the date of our marriage. With a licence, it took five days and the cost was seven and sixpence. After that, he took me to his flat and, after inspecting it and doing some measuring and debating over décor (fortunately we had very similar tastes), we hit the shops, as I didn't want to move into a bachelor pad. We chose a new three-piece suite, curtains, rugs and bedding, and we spent the next four days turning the flat into our home.

I woke up on the morning of the wedding and decided to tell Mummy of my plans. I made her some tea and went into the bedroom. Daddy had gone out by now.

'Come on, Mummy, wake up. I have something to tell you. Drink your tea.'

But she stubbornly turned over and said, 'Leave me to sleep!'

So I dressed in my black suit and pink chiffon blouse – yes, I was getting married in black! I also had the big, black cartwheel hat that I had worn to my cousin's wedding in Nottingham. I knew the moment had gone for me to tell Mummy and I angrily kicked the hat through the front door, which I quietly closed from the outside. I stuck the hat on my head and crept quietly down the stairs, but when I reached the pavement outside, I ran like hell was on my heels.

Johnnie's father and stepmother were at the register office, along with our friends Pam and Ray, who was the best man, and my father's sister Dora, who by that point was living near Brighton and whom I had confided in about the wedding. I cried throughout the ceremony and the handkerchief given to me by Aunt Dora was covered with mascara.

Once we were married, the reality hit that now it was time to face the music. We went into the bar opposite the register office and Johnnie knew he had to phone my mother and take control. After sitting me down with yet another glass of Champagne (I was becoming a bit of a Champagne Charlie!), he went to use the public phone in the bar. He returned, grinning, and said, 'I told your mother that we just got married and she said to come straight over.'

Looking puzzled, he added that she didn't seem all that surprised. I turned to Aunt Dora. 'Did you tell her?'

'No, of course I didn't, Eva.' It was so like Mummy to have guessed what was going on but say nothing about it, leaving me to make my own decision.

Mummy had told Johnnie to bring the whole wedding party, so we piled into taxis again. As soon as we entered the flat, Mummy hugged me and I burst out crying again, feeling guilt, relief and happiness all rolled into one. Nathan rushed out saying, 'Going for some Champagne, back soon.' The twins bounced around with excitement. Only my father wasn't really talking, and certainly not being friendly to Johnnie.

Mummy took Johnnie's arm and guided him into the kitchen, away from everyone. She explained about the Romany blessing, which I had already told him about. They were in there for about twenty minutes and were laughing like old friends, which they did quickly become. Mummy liked him and approved. She felt that he had something very important in common with our family: the same sense of humour. She admitted to him that she had sensed that morning that I'd be returning a married woman.

But despite how well they hit it off, I suspect that, while in the kitchen, she still did what Romany elders traditionally do when talking to the bridegroom, and told Johnnie that if he didn't look after me he'd get his bollocks chopped off!

The blessing was a merry affair, helped by the

amount of Champagne we'd all drunk. Mummy pricked our thumbs and held them together, and then she bound our hands together with a dickler. She popped down to the garden to find an evergreen branch, which she broke in two and gave us half each. Then she filled a silver fruit bowl with water and lit a fire in her trifle dish. Johnnie had to tread over both, showing he would go through fire and water for me.

We were truly married. We told everyone we were going on honeymoon – 'Mind your own business' was our reply when asked where – but in fact we just wanted to go back to Johnnie's flat.

Mummy suddenly said, 'What clothes did you take with you this morning?'

'Just what I'm standing up in,' I admitted.

She insisted on helping me pack for my honeymoon. As we folded clothes into a suitcase, she said thoughtfully, 'I must have known something was up when I gave you the bracelet.' I had received the traditional Romany dowry five days before my wedding, on the very day I decided to marry Johnnie.

Finally we were able to leave, and as we headed back to Johnnie's flat in a taxi, I felt sure this was the beginning of the happiest time in my life.

Epilogue

'So come on, Eva, where are we going?' Johnnie challenged me.

'What do you mean?' It was 10.30 p.m. and I all I was thinking about was going to bed.

'I know you,' he said smiling. 'Your foot's tapping away and that means you need to get away. So where are we going?'

'Blackpool,' I declared, laughing. I hadn't consciously thought about it, but Johnnie could always read me and my needs, and he was right. I wanted to see Daisy and Honour.

'Pack,' he commanded and disappeared.

Fifteen minutes later, he was back. 'The car's ready,' he said. He'd put our mattress in the back of our estate car and made a bed with blankets and pillows. He carried out the sleeping children: our oldest boy Warren, who was five, Bradley, who was four, Gregory, three, and our baby daughter Claire. With the birth of my little girl, I'd felt my life was truly complete. I'd wanted to call her Eva, but Johnnie felt there were enough Evas in our family.

'Shhh, go back to sleep,' he said as he tucked them up. 'And we'll be in Blackpool in time for breakfast.'

As the car pulled out into the quiet streets, I felt truly blessed. I couldn't give my children the traditional Romany life, but I could give them parents who loved each other, and them, very much. And I could give them the excitement and anticipation I remembered as a child of wondering, as I dropped off to sleep, where we'd wake up tomorrow. My children experienced this many times and, believe me, they loved it too.

Acknowledgements

This book was written for all my Romany family so that we may never forget our roots. I want to thank my daughter Claire for the tremendous help she gave me with putting my story into words – I could never have done it without you. Thank you also to my son Warren for all his help and guidance. I would like to thank Bradley and Gregory for their support and encouragement, as well as Shunty and John Taylor for helping me remember things and for letting me use their photographs. Honour and Daisy were also great at helping jog my memory, and their brother Johnnie Heron very kindly let me use many of his photographs. Finally, thanks to my editors Ingrid Connell and Lorraine Green at Pan Macmillan for their guidance, help and patience.

extracts reading groups
competitions books new
discounts extracts
competitions
books new
events b
extracts
new
intervi
events ex
disco
new boo
event
discounts extrac

extracts events reading groups
competitions books extracts new